SEE HOW THEY RUN

RUN

A Farce in Three Acts

by Philip King

D1511032

A SAMUEL FRENCH ACTING EDITION

SAMUEL FRENCH

FOUNDED 1830

New York Hollywood London Toronto

SAMUELFRENCH.COM

SEE HOW THEY RUN

STORY OF THE PLAY

No question about the title of this smash London hit. So swift in the action, so involved the situations, so rib-tickling the plot that at its finish audiences are left as exhausted from laughter as though they themselves had run a footrace. Galloping in and out of the four doors of an English Vicarage are an American actor and actress (he is now stationed with the Air Force in England), a cockney maid who has seen too many American movies, an old maid who "touches alcohol for the first time in her life," four men in clergyman's suits presenting the problem of which is which, for disguised as one is an escaped prisoner, and another a sedate bishop aghast at all these goings on and the trumped-up stories that are told him. Said "Theatre World" an English publication when the play was first produced in London : "An apt title for an excellent farce of the most involved variety . . . Nor is there any offense anywhere in this admirably written play which deserves a long run for its rollicking good humor."

. Program of first American production of "SEE HOW THEY RUN" as presented by Actors' Theatre '49, Plainfield, N. J. on May 11th, 1949.

SEE HOW THEY RUN

A Farce by Phillip King

CAST
In Order of Appearance

IDA (a Maid) .... *Constance Kelly*
MISS SKILLON .... *Doris Smith*
THE REVEREND LIONEL TOOP .... *John Willis*
PENELOPE TOOP *(his wife)* .... *Judy Lambert*
CORPORAL CLIVE WINTON .... *Harvé Clement*
THE INTRUDER .... *Richard Warren*
THE BISHOP OF LAX .... *Zack Waters*
THE REVEREND ARTHUR HUMPHREY .. *Tom Leggett*
SERGEANT TOWERS .... *Charles C. Welch*

PRODUCTION UNDER THE DIRECTION OF
TOM TAGGART

TECHNICAL DIRECTOR .... *William Corio*
STAGE MANAGER .... *Constance Kelly*
HOUSE MANAGER .... *Mark Smith, Jr.*

SYNOPSIS OF SCENES

The Action Takes Place in the Hall at the Vicarage,
Merton-Cum-Middlewick

ACT. I:—An Afternoon in September

ACT. II:—The Same Night

ACT. III:—A Few Minutes Later

Produced by Special Arrangement with Samuel French

See How They Run

ACT ONE

SCENE.—*The pleasantly furnished Hall in the Vicarage at Merton-cum-Middlewick, a small village in England.*

There is a staircase running up the L. wall, and a door, down L., leading to the front door and the kitchen. Back C., large French windows opening on to a lovely garden. The dining-room door is up R., and the fireplace is down R. A large sofa or settee R.C., with a table behind it, on which is the telephone. There is a small table down R., below the fireplace. Another table L.C., with a chair on the Left of it. The table is set for tea. In the L. wall, below the stairs, a large closet. On the R. of the stairs, a large chest. On the R. of this, an armchair. A stool down L. below door.

As the CURTAIN *rises, a female voice is heard from upstairs. It is* PENELOPE TOOP *in the bathroom, doing her singing exercises. She runs up and down various scales with wild abandon, occasionally dwelling on a top note and* "Ning-ning-nong-no"-*ing on it.*

While this is going on, IDA, *the maid, stands at* L.C., *adjusting the tea-things on the tray, with askance glances towards the "singing."* IDA *is a plain but likeable village girl about eighteen years of age. She goes to the stairs, waiting for a lull in the scales.*

When the lull arrives:

IDA *(shouting upstairs).* TEA! *(But the scales have*

5

started again. Trying to stop PENELOPE) TEA!!
(Having failed, she addresses the room.) Owisantsheor-
ful. *(meaning "Oh, isn't she awful!" She begins to
ascend the staircase, but when halfway up, the front-
DOORBELL rings. She turns and comes down again,
muttering resignedly.)* Woman's work is never done!
(She exits down L. *There is a murmur of voices, then:
Off stage.)* Come this way, Miss Skillon. *(She re-
enters, followed by* MISS SKILLON, *a large rather sour
spinster of thirty-five.)*

MISS SKILLON *(as she enters).* Thank you, Ida!

IDA *(dolefully).* Don't mention it'm! (MISS SKILLON
starts. IDA *ascends the stairs.)* I'll tell Mrs. Toop you're
here'm.

MISS SKILLON *(crossing to below the sofa* R.C.*).*
You need not . . .

IDA *(pausing on the stairs).* She's in the bathroom.

MISS SKILLON. There is no need to . . .

IDA. Bathing.

MISS SKILLON. Will you let me speak, girl? There
is no need to disturb Mrs. Toop. I want to see the
Vicar.

IDA. Ow! He's in the garden.

MISS SKILLON. Well, will you . . .

IDA. Gard'nin'!

MISS SKILLON *(sits on sofa).* Tell him I'm here,
will you?

IDA *(crossing to the french windows).* Okydokey!

MISS SKILLON. Okydokey! *(Moving down* R.*)* What
an expression!

IDA *(returning to* L.C., *giggling).* I know! Is-an-tit-
torful? I get it from her!

MISS SKILLON. Her! Whom?

IDA. Mrs. Toop. *(Another giggle.)* She's a caution!

MISS SKILLON *(severely).* Ida! That will do. After
you have told the Vicar I am here, put my bicycle round
in the garage. I think we're going to have some rain.

IDA. Yes, Miss Skillon. *(She moves to the French windows.)*

MISS SKILLON. And, Ida! *(IDA turns.)* Don't ride it, wheel it.

IDA. Yes'm.

(She exits through the windows. MISS SKILLON then "noses" round the room. The singing is still going on upstairs. MISS SKILLON does not like it. She rubs a finger on the table behind the settee, searching for dust, and finds it. She "tut! tuts!" loudly; then crosses to the table L.C. and peeps under the lid of the muffin-dish. The REVEREND LIONEL TOOP's voice is heard in the garden.)

LIONEL *(off stage)*. Oh, very well, Ida. (MISS SKILLON *re-seats herself hastily on the sofa R.C. Off stage.)* I didn't know you could ride a bicycle, Ida! (MISS SKILLON *rises, furious, but sees LIONEL as he enters through the French windows. The REVEREND LIONEL TOOP is a man of thirty-six, of medium height, pleasant faced, though of somewhat staid expression. He wears a black suit. As he moves from C. to the tea-table.)* Good afternoon, Miss Skillon! I'm so sorry I wasn't in to receive you. Penelope didn't mention that you were coming to tea.

MISS SKILLON. I have not come to tea, Mr. Toop. I wanted to see *you.*

LIONEL. Oh! Oh, yes, certainly. *(Seeing the tea.)* But tea is here, so won't you join us? *(Then, before* MISS SKILLON *can speak.)* Do sit down. (MISS SKILLON *sits on sofa. He crosses to the bottom of the staircase, calling.)* PENELOPE! *(But the scales are loud and high.)* PENELOPE! *(A pause.)* No use! When Penelope begins her exercises, she's lost to the world! Never mind! We'll begin, shall we? *(He crosses to the table* L.C. *and begins to pour tea.)*

MISS SKILLON *(solemnly)*. Mr. Toop, I am hurt!

LIONEL *(vaguely)*. Oh dear! Where?

MISS SKILLON. I am hurt—*grieved!*

LIONEL. I am sorry, Miss Skillon. I'm afraid I I cannot offer you sugar.

MISS SKILLON (*witheringly*). *No tea*, thank you! Mr. Toop, I would be grateful if you could give me your undivided attention for just five minutes!

LIONEL. Five minutes. Why, of course, Miss Skillon. Certainly. Five minutes.

(Unconsciously, he takes his watch from his waistcoat pocket and places it on the table, as he has so often done in the pulpit. MISS SKILLON re-acts to this.)

MISS SKILLON (*sharply*). It's the church decorations for the Harvest Festival.

LIONEL (*helping himself to a muffin*). What is?

MISS SKILLON (*after a glare*). Mr. Toop, have you been dissatisfied with my contribution to the Church decorations in the past?

LIONEL (*to L. of the table*). No, no, I don't think so. *(Sitting.)* Why?

MISS SKILLON. You will member that I have always decorated the pulpit for the Easter and Harvest Festivals. It has always been understood that the pulpit was my special little effort. Everyone knows it! I have decorated the pulpit since—since . . .

LIONEL (*thoughtlessly*). Since time immemorial, I know!

MISS SKILLON (*acidly*). Not *quite* so long as that, Mr. Toop!

LIONEL. No, no, of course not, Miss Skillon. Do go on!

MISS SKILLON. This afternoon I arrive at the church to do my little bit, and what do I find? *(A pause.)* The pulpit has already been decorated, behind my back!

(PENELOPE's singing begins again off stage.)

LIONEL. No! Who has dared to do such a thing?

MISS SKILLON. No one would tell me, but I have my suspicions. *(The scales have now given way to modern humming. PENELOPE sings the first two lines. The rest is more or less "la-la'd." MISS SKILLON looks towards the stairs exasperated, then at LIONEL, who smiles apologetically. Trying to ignore the singing.)* I have no quarrel with you, Mr. Toop. We have always been—er—the best of friends. Have we not?

LIONEL. Oh yes, undoubtedly! Do have some tea? *(He offers her a cup.)*

MISS SKILLON. No, thank you. *(Waving it away—with a sigh.)* Wonderful friends. *(Rather markedly.)* *Everyone* knows that! So I hope what I am going to say . . . (PENELOPE *is now reaching for a top A which turns out to be a flat one.* MISS SKILLON *looks round furiously, then back to the Vicar with a sickly smile.)* I—I find it very difficult to concentrate—er—with that dreadful noise—your dear wife singing. *(She waves a hand stairwards.)*

LIONEL. Yes, it is a little distracting. *(Rising.)* I'll ask her to . . . *(He crosses to the staircase.)* Penelope! PENELOPE!

(The singing stops.)

PENELOPE *(off stage)*. Oh! Is that you, Lionel?

LIONEL. Yes, my dear . . .

PENELOPE. Ask Ida to bring the tea in, will you?

LIONEL. Tea is already in.

PENELOPE. Oh! *(Then quickly.)* Go easy with the muffins!

LIONEL. Penelope! Miss Skillon is here!

PENELOPE. Who?

LIONEL. Miss Skillon.

PENELOPE. What about her?

LIONEL. She's here.

PENELOPE. Oh!

LIONEL. Do hurry down, dear. Miss Skillon is hurt!

PENELOPE. Good—I mean I'm terribly sorry.

(LIONEL *comes down the stairs again, to above the table*
L.C.)

LIONEL. Such a keen sense of humor! *(With as-
sumed brightness.)* Now, Miss Skillon! Where were
we? Oh, yes! Of course! The pulpit! *(He picks up his
watch.)*

MISS SKILLON. Mr. Toop, I will come straight to the
point. I have reason to believe that the pulpit was
decorated—behind my back—by Mrs. Toop!

LIONEL. Oh! Dear, dear, dear, dear, dear. Yes . . . er
. . . most awkward!

MISS SKILLON. Of course, I have nothing against
Mrs. Toop personally. Nothing at all! There are some
who do not think it *quite* the thing for the Vicar's wife
to appear in the village wearing trousers, even in these
times, but as I say we *must* remember that Mrs. Toop
was an actress—an American actress before she married you!

LIONEL. Mrs. Toop was also the niece of a bishop
before *I* married *her,* Miss Skillon—and still is!

MISS SKILLON *(hastily).* Oh yes, indeed; I know. But
of course the stage! A curious profession!

(PENELOPE TOOP *appears at the top of the stairs. She
is a pretty young woman of twenty-five. She wears
fluffy slippers and an exotic kimono.)*

PENELOPE *(as she runs down the stairs).* Miss
Skillon! *(Gaily, as she comes to the tea-wagon.)* You
must forgive this *(indicating her kimono),* Miss Skillon,
but I'm straight from the bath.

MISS SKILLON. Of course, Mrs. Toop. One does
get so dirty decorating the church, doesn't one?

PENELOPE. Quate-quate, quate. *(To L of the table.)*
Well, now who has been "mother"?

MISS SKILLON. Mother?

PENELOPE. I mean, who poured out the tea? *(Sitting.)*
I'm dying for a cup, but I'm frightfully superstitious.

The English say if two people pour out of the same pot, it's a sign of a row.

MISS SKILLON. Oh!

PENELOPE. Or that one of the pourers is going to have a baby. And we don't want one yet. Do we Lionel?

LIONEL. Penelope! Please!

PENELOPE. And I'm sure Miss Skillon doesn't!

MISS SKILLON *(shocked)*. Mrs. Toop ! ! !

LIONEL *(quickly)*. I poured. *(He pours tea for* PENELOPE.*)*

PENELOPE *(airily)*. By the way, darling, do you think Mr. "What's-his-name" will mind?

LIONEL. Mr. Who? *(Handing her a cup.)* Really, Penelope, you do . . .

PENELOPE. Oh, you know, darling. Mr. . . . er—your friend who is taking the service for you to-morrow.

LIONEL. You mean Humphrey?

PENELOPE. Yes, of course, Mr. Humphrey.

LIONEL. Mr. Humphrey is not a friend of mine, Penelope. I have never even met the man.

PENELOPE. Well, do you think he'll mind?

LIONEL. Will he mind what?

PENELOPE. Well, darling, we ran rather short of chrysanthemums. I'm afraid the pulpit is mostly decorated with turnips and leeks! ! (LIONEL *looks uneasily towards* MISS SKILLON. PENELOPE *notices this and rises.)* Now, Miss Skillon, more tea.

MISS SKILLON. I do not wish any tea, thank you!

PENELOPE. Oh! *(There is a strained silence.)* What have I done wrong now?

LIONEL. Penelope!

PENELOPE. It's no use pretending that I haven't erred and strayed! The air is simply charged with righteous indignation. So, Lionel, will you run away like a good boy, then Miss Skillon and I can both let our back hair down and scratch each other's eyes out.

MISS SKILLON. I did not call to see you, Mrs. Toop. I merely wished to have a little talk with the Vicar.

PENELOPE. It is a most exasperating fact, Miss

Skillon, that after every one of your "little talks" with my husband, he and I have one hell of a row.

LIONEL *(above and L. of the table)*. Penelope dear, I am sure Miss Skillon only wishes to be helpful. She has known the villagers longer than you have. She hears more of their gossip than you do.

PENELOPE (C.) I'll say she does!

MISS SKILLON *(rising)*. Mr. Toop, I cannot stay here to be insulted. Mrs. Toop, you have been in this village nearly a year now. During all that time, I have never done anything but try to befriend you.

PENELOPE *(with a sigh)*. Then it must be my fault. *(Crosses to C.)* I'm sorry, Miss Skillon, but the fact remains that every time we meet, I am seized with a wild desire to leap on the village green, tear off all my clothes, and dance the Hula-Hula!

MISS SKILLON. If you did, we might be shocked, Mrs. Toop, but I don't think we should be surprised. *(turns away R.)*

PENELOPE. By the way, what is it this time? The soldier in the Jeep?

LIONEL. No, Penelope, it is not. As a matter of fact Miss Skillon mentioned that—to me yesterday. It was a most unfortunate incident.

PENELOPE *(to LIONEL)*. You call waving to a soldier in a Jeep an unfortunate incident?

MISS SKILLON. It is what others might call it that matters, Mrs. Toop. You not only waved, you—er—"yoo-hoo'ed."

PENELOPE. "Yoo-hoo'ed"?—So I did!

LIONEL *(to above the table)*. Did you know the soldier, Penelope?

PENELOPE. Not from *Adam*. In fact, I hardly had time to notice him. He just waved and "yoo-hoo'ed," so I just waved and "yoo-hoo'ed" back *(Sweetly.)* Didn't I, Miss Skillon?

LIONEL. Hardly conduct suitable for a Vicar's wife. surely?

PENELOPE. I'm sorry, darling, but there are times

when I forget that I am a Vicar's wife and behave like an ordinary human being.

LIONEL. Penelope, I resent that. I . . .

PENELOPE. Lionel, if we're going to have a row, we are not going to have it in front of Miss Skillon. *(on stair landing).*

MISS SKILLON. You need not worry about me, Mrs. Toop. I am going. *(Dropping a glove.)* I am sorry my good intentions have been so misunderstood. . . Good-bye, Mr. Toop.

LIONEL *(moving to her).* Miss Skillon, I can't say how . . .

MISS SKILLON. Please! Don't think about it, Mr. Toop. I hope I can forget and forgive. *(She stoops to pick up her glove.)* I think I'm broad-minded.

PENELOPE. I'm sure you are, Miss Skillon.

LIONEL *(sharply).* Penelope! *(Then to* MISS SKILLON.*)* I'll see you to your . . . er . . . bicycle.

MISS SKILLON. Thank you, I'm perfectly capable of mounting by myself.

(She crosses to the French windows, followed by LIONEL. *They exit. After they are off,* PENELOPE *runs her hands through her hair, then half shouts, half screams.)*

PENELOPE. Yah! *(She crosses quickly to the door down* L. *Calling.)* Ida!

IDA *(entering down* L.*).* Yes'm?

PENELOPE. You can clear away the tea things, Ida.

IDA. Yes'm. *(Putting the things on the tray.)* Somebody 'asn't drunk all their tea!

PENELOPE. You can take it away. It's mine. I don't want it.

IDA *(lifting the lid of the muffin-dish).* An' you 'aven't 'ad no muffin! You 'aven't been lettin' 'er upset you, 'ave you'm? You know why she's got 'er knife into you, dont you'm?

PENELOPE. I think so, Ida.

IDA. An' so does everybody. Well, I'll say this for 'er—she tried 'ard enough, but if she had landed 'im, it would 'ave been "Gawd 'elp 'im!"

(She exits with the tea-tray down L. LIONEL *re-enters at the French windows.)*

LIONEL *(moving to* C.*)*. Penelope, I'm ashamed! Ashamed!

PENELOPE. I knew it! I knew it! Off we go! Ooooh! One day I'll strangle that woman. What did she actually come up about? I never did find out.

LIONEL. It appears that you have decorated the pulpit for the Harvest Festival.

PENELOPE. Well, what about it?

LIONEL. The pulpit has always been Miss Skillon's territory.

PENELOPE. Oh, darling! Lionel, I didn't do it purposely, I swear I didn't. Of course, that old cow will never believe it.

LIONEL. Penelope, I must ask you to moderate your language. You know in your position, you should behave with a little more—er—decorum.

PENELOPE. You mean I should *act* the Vicar's wife a little more?

LIONEL. Not "act," but *be* the the Vicar's wife. *(To* L. *of the sofa.)* That is the trouble, Penelope. Can't you forget that you have been an actress and behave more as befits the niece of a Bishop?

PENELOPE *(flaring)*. And just *how* is that? The only other Bishop's niece I know is in the chorus.

LIONEL. I believe you are deliberately trying to provoke me. May I ask you just one question? Is it absolutely necessary for you to go about the village in trousers?

PENELOPE. Why on earth shouldn't I? They're comfortable, and serviceable. *And* they're economical.

LIONEL. That may be, but as Miss Skillon says, they . . .

PENELOPE. Darling, a woman with a bottom like hers could say anything.

LIONEL. Penelope! *(He turns away up C.)*

PENELOPE. She's only livid because she can't wear them.

LIONEL *(crosses L.C.)*. I refuse to stay here and listen to your vulgarity. Oh, and another thing . . .

(IDA *enters down* L.)

IDA. Please, sir.

LIONEL. What is it, Ida?

IDA *(to L. of the table L.C.)*. It's Willie Briggs from the farm. He's waiting at the back door.

LIONEL. I'll see him at once. *(He crosses to the door L. and turns.)* May I suggest, Penelope, that you go upstairs and dress? I would rather people saw you in trousers than without them.

(He stamps off down L. PENELOPE sighs, takes a magazine from the pile on the table and crosses towards the settee.)

IDA *(turning at the door L., mysteriously)*. She's still 'ere'm!

PENELOPE. Who are you talking about, Ida?

IDA. Miss Skillon'm. She in the garage. *(crosses to C.)*

PENELOPE. What *is* she doing there?

IDA. Mendin' 'er bicycle. I punctured it.

PENELOPE. Purposely?

IDA. No'm. For spite.

(She exits to the kitchen. PENELOPE is about to sit when TELEPHONE rings. She crosses to it.)

PENELOPE *(at the 'phone)* Hullo—hullo——This is the Vicarage. Mrs. Toop speaking . . . who? *(Delighted.)* Uncle! Uncle Dudley! How lovely! Where are you speaking from? . . . Badcaster? . . . What on earth are you doing there? . . . Coming on here? . . . Why, of course . . . We shall be delighted . . . To-morrow? . . . But why not to-night? . . . I see. Well, make it as early as possible in the morning . . . Why not? I see. (LIONEL *re-enters down* L.). You're a wicked old man . . . *(With a look at* LIONEL.) But you take an awful lot of living up to! . . . No, I can't explain now. It would take too long . . . See you to-morrow. Good-bye! . . . *(She takes the magazine and sits sofa.)*

LIONEL. Who was that?

PENELOPE *(flippantly)*. Uncle!

LIONEL. Uncle who?

PENELOPE. Uncle Dudley.

LIONEL *(excitedly)*. Not . . . *not* the *Bishop?*

PENELOPE. Himself.

LIONEL *(flustered)*. Gracious! What . . . I . . . er . . . what was that you said about seeing him to-morrow?

PENELOPE *(shortly)*. Lionel, there's no need for you to get so excited. He's staying the night in Badcaster at the "Cross Keys" and coming on here to-morrow.

LIONEL. The "Cross Keys"? But that's such an indifferent hotel, but I suppose he wouldn't know that.

PENELOPE. Even a Bishop can learn.

LIONEL *(bitterly)*. The Bishop here to-morrow and I'm not taking the service. *(He sits on the sofa)*.

PENELOPE. I know! Aren't you lucky?

LIONEL. I beg your pardon.

PENELOPE. Darling, Uncle is very proud of the fact that he memorizes his sermons. If he saw you *reading* yours, he'd cut me out of his will! In any case, he's purposely arriving just in time to be too late for the morning service.

LIONEL. Extraordinary!

PENELOPE *(rising)*. No, "human." *(She goes to the cupboard up* R.) Do you think we can get something decent in for Uncle to drink? All we have at the moment is a bottle of very bad cooking-sherry. *(Producing a bottle from the cupboard.)*

LIONEL. What shall we get?

PENELOPE *(to the table)*. Anything you can. Use your sex appeal. Uncle is very broadminded.

LIONEL. I'll get what I can. Oh dear! *(Rising.)* I wonder if I should go now!

PENELOPE. Go where?

LIONEL. To Wathampton, with the Glee Singers. They are giving a concert at the American Air Base, to-night. Young Briggs has just come to tell me their pianist is ill, and, as they cannot find anyone else, to ask if I will deputize for him.

PENELOPE. Well, why shouldn't you?

LIONEL *(crossing to* C.). But with the Bishop arriving to-morrow . . . and as I have never met him . . .

PENELOPE. I don't think there is any necessity for you to "prepare" yourself for the occasion! Off you go and enjoy yourself. *(She goes into the cupboard* L. *and returns with his coat, hat, scarf and umbrella.)*

LIONEL. I should hardly describe playing the piano for the Glee Singers as enjoying myself. However, I suppose I must do it. Briggs is waiting for me, now.

PENELOPE *(helping him on with his things)*. Will you be late back, darling?

LIONEL. I shouldn't think so, although Briggs said something about a supper after the concert. Apparently that is the principal feature of the evening.

(IDA enters down L. *She is now dressed to go out.)*

IDA. Please, sir, Willie Briggs says will you hurry, sir. Time's getting on.

LIONEL. All right. I'm just coming. *(To* PENELOPE.) You're sure you won't be lonely, darling?

PENELOPE. Good heavens, no! Why should I?

LIONEL. H'm well. Good-bye, Penelope. *(He kisses her lightly.)* You will go upstairs and put a few more clothes on, won't you? *(Turning to* IDA.) Your night out, Ida?

IDA. Yes, sir.

(Exit LIONEL *down* L.)

PENELOPE *(moving to* C.*)*. Ida, when you come to-night, put a couple of hot-water bottles in the spare-room bed, will you? We have a guest arriving to-morrow.

IDA. Oh'm?

PENELOPE. My uncle. The Bishop of Lax.

IDA. A Bishop!

PENELOPE. And, Ida, don't be late in. You know the Vicar doesn't like you out after ten. Americans or no Americans.

(She runs up the staircase and off L. IDA *crosses* R. *to the mantel mirror, takes a wretched-looking powder-puff from her bag, dabs her face vigorously, then surveys the result in the mirror.)*

IDA *(dolefully)*. The trouble with you, Ida, is, you 'aven't got no "oomph!" *(She stoops to adjust her shoelace.* MISS SKILLON *appears at the French window and comes in somewhat furtively. She does not notice* IDA, *but* IDA *notices her. She watches* MISS SKILLON *for a moment. Then.)* Was you wantin' anything'm?

MISS SKILLON *(starting)*. Oh! I didn't see you there, Ida.

IDA *(down* R.*)*. I saw you.

MISS SKILLON. I suppose you know you have punctured my bicycle?

IDA *(with questioning innocence)*. Oh'm I never?

MISS SKILLON. You're a very careless girl. I wondered if the Vicar would help me. I'm having a little trouble with my inner tube.

IDA. I'm sure he'd be delighted, but he's gone out.

MISS SKILLON. Out! Where?

IDA. Out!!

MISS SKILLON. Has Mrs. Toop gone too?

IDA. No, she 'asn't. *(Warningly.)* She'll be down in a minute.

MISS SKILLON. Oh, well . . . in that case I won't stay.

(She moves to R. of the windows again, but stops as
CORPORAL CLIVE WINTON *appears there from off* L.
CLIVE *is a handsome young man, wearing uniform of
Corporal in the U. S. Air Forces.)*

CLIVE. Good afternoon.

MISS SKILLON *(frigidly)*. Good afternoon!

IDA *(not to be left out)*. Good afternoon!

MISS SKILLON *(sharply)*. Ida, is this a friend of yours?

IDA. No'm! *(Then optimistically.)* Not yet!

CLIVE *(to* MISS SKILLON). Excuse me, are you Mrs. . . . er are you the Vicar's wife?

MISS SKILLON. I am not.

CLIVE. Good—I mean, well it doesn't really matter . . . what I mean . . . *(He steps further into the room.)*

MISS SKILLON. Did you want to see Mrs. Toop?

CLIVE. Mrs. who?

MISS SKILLON. Mrs. Toop. The Vicar's wife. Do you want to see her?

CLIVE *(up* L.C.). I don't really know.

MISS SKILLON. I beg your pardon.

CLIVE. As a matter of fact, I'm trying to find a young lady.

MISS SKILLON. Indeed!

IDA. Do you mean a *special* one or would *any* one do?

MISS SKILLON. Ida!

CLIVE *(laughing)*. Oh! A special one. A very special one. A very old friend of mine.

MISS SKILLON. Why come to the vicarage? There are no young ladies here. None!

IDA *(hurt)*. Well, I may not be what you'd call a "lady," but I've got me feelings!

MISS SKILLON. Quiet, Ida! Haven't I seen you before, young man?

CLIVE. Seen me before? No, I don't think so.

MISS SKILLON. I'm sure I've seen your face before. I have a very good memory for faces.

CLIVE. I've had it a long time. *(Crosses to R. PENELOPE appears on the staircase. She now wears slacks. She begins to descend, but on seeing CLIVE she stops. Turning, and seeing PENELOPE.)* Penelope!

PENELOPE. Clive!

CLIVE. Sweetheart!!

PENELOPE. Darling! *(She rushes down the stairs and straight into CLIVE's open arms. MISS SKILLON watches, aghast. Still in his arms.)* What *are* you doing here?

CILVE. Looking for you.

PENELOPE. This is heaven! *(Then noticing MISS SKILLON.)* Oh, Miss Skillon! *(Then, pointedly.)* The Vicar is out.

MISS SKILLON *(goggling)*. I . . . er . . . I . . .

PENELOPE *(sweeping on)*. I'm afraid he won't be back until rather late.

MISS SKILLON. But . . . I . . .

PENELOPE. I'll tell him you called . . . again . . . Also that you will no doubt call again, *very early* in the morning.

MISS SKILLON. But . . . I . . .

PENELOPE. I think that is all, Miss Skillon.

(MISS SKILLON is left with no alternative but to go. She does this through the windows, reluctantly.)

MISS SKILLON *(as she goes)*. Well really . . .! *(She exits.)*

(CLIVE moves to C.)

PENELOPE *(intending to get rid of IDA)*. *Oh, Ida! . . . I . . .* This is an old friend of mine. We used to be on the stage together.

IDA *(moving towards the kitchen)*. S'alright'm. You don't have to use a sledge hammer to get rid of *me*. *(Crossing to the door: smiling sweetly at them both.)*

"Live an' let live," that's what I say. *(She exits down L.)*

CLIVE. Well, you certainly got rid of them in a hurry. But weren't you abrupt with the—Camp Fire Girl?

PENELOPE. Miss Skillon? *(To L. of the sofa.)* Every time I see that woman my temperature rises and breaks another record. Never mind her, though it's a pity I embraced you in front of her.

CILVE *(below the settee)*. Why?

PENELOPE. She won't sleep until she's told my husband.

CLIVE *(surprised)*. Your husband? I say, you're *not* Mrs. Boop-a-doop, are you?

PENELOPE. "Toop," darling, "Toop." *(Sits arm of sofa)* Don't make it worse than it is!

CLIVE. But you're *not*, are you?

PENELOPE. I am — and have been for nearly a year now.

CLIVE. But why?

PENELOPE. What do you mean, "why"?

CLIVE. Well, you—a Vicar's wife. The last time I saw you, you were a young actress bursting with ambition and now you're here, living in England.

PENELOPE. An old married hag?

CILVE. No, not yet.

PENELOPE. There's no mystery about it, Clive. I knew Lionel, that's my husband, when I was a child. We played together. Then my family moved to America. Eighteen months ago, when I came over with the U. S. O. we met again, fell in love, and—here I am!

CLIVE. But your career?

PENELOPE. Oh, that! My acting wasn't what you'd call brilliant, was it?

CLIVE. Oh, I don't know. Not too bad. Are you happy here?

PENELOPE. Perfectly. Although sometimes I lose my sense of humor and want to scream the place down!

CILVE. I bet you do.

PENELOPE. But what about you? What are you doing here in uniform? By the way, would you like some tea?

CILVE. No thanks.

PENELOPE. Sorry I can't offer you anything else, except cooking sherry.

CILVE. I haven't brought anything to — cook.

PENELOPE. Tell me about yourself.

CLIVE. Well, thanks to our Russian friends, my discharge hasn't yet come through. I've just been sent here from Berlin.

PENELOPE. Sent where?

CLIVE. Wathampton. The air base there. Very unimportant job on the Air Lift to Berlin.

PENELOPE. Wathampton. Lionel has gone there for the evening. He's playing the piano for the village Glee Singers. They're giving a concert for the Americans.

CLIVE. Poor Americans.

PENELOPE. Clive, tell me, how did you know *I* was here?

CILVE. I saw you yesterday.

PENELOPE. When?

CILVE. You saw me, too. I was in a Jeep. I thought you recognized me. I waved and "yoo-hoo'ed." You waved back.

PENELOPE *(laughing)*. Good Lord! Was that *you?*

CILVE. Yes. I saw you turn in at the gate here, and thought perhaps you were staying at the Vicarage, so, as I had the afternoon off, I thought I'd look you up.

PENELOPE. Thank goodness you did, Clive, I was just wondering what I was going to do to pass the evening. All the same, I don't think we ought to stay in the house. *(Rises)*.

CLIVE. Why not? It's a very comfortable house.

PENELOPE. Yes, but—except for you—I am completely alone in it.

CLIVE. H'm! I see. And Miss — er — Skillon wouldn't approve, eh? *(He rises.)*

PENELOPE. She wouldn't approve, but would she love it. God! What she'd make of it!!

CLIVE. Then we'd better go out somewhere. *(Up c.)*

PENELOPE. Yes, but where? There's nowhere *to go* round here.

CLIVE. We can always go to the—I suppose it wouldn't be quite the thing for the Vicar's wife to be seen in the village pub with an American soldier.

PENELOPE. It wouldn't be quite the thing for the Vicar's wife to be seen in the pub at all, you fool! *(After a pause.)* We might go to a movie. *(Suddenly.)* Wait a minute! *(She rises, crosses to the table down R., and hunts for a newspaper.)* Could you bear to put your nose inside a theatre, or would it break your heart?

CILVE. A theatre? What theatre?

PENELOPE. We have a little theatre group. *(Having searched the paper.)* Here we are! *(Reading.)* "This week the Court Players present . . ." *(She breaks off.)* NO! I can't believe it!

CLIVE. I can. Six to four it's "Sweeney Tod."

PENELOPE. Listen! *(She reads.)* "This week the Court Players present Noel Coward's delightful comedy, PRIVATE LIVES!!!"

CLIVE *(laughing and incredulous)*. NO!!!

PENELOPE *(also laughing)*. YES!!! Clive, just *how* many weeks did we tour "Private Lives" for the U. S. O.?

CLIVE. Forty-three—— Oh, and a half! There were those last three nights at Merthyr-Tydfil.

PENELOPE. Could you *bear* to see it, to-night?

CLIVE. Bear to! I'd love to! Though I'd probably be thrown out of the theatre for shouting out the lines of my old part.

PENELOPE. Then we'll go.

CLIVE. Half a minute! Where is this?

PENELOPE. Blatford. It's only a few miles away and there's a bus.

CILVE. Sorry, my dear. The trip's off.

PENELOPE. What? Why?

CILVE. Blatford is out of bounds.

PENELOPE. What does that mean?

CLIVE. Simply that if I was caught in Blatford in uniform, I should be shot at dawn *and* they'd cancel my next leave.

PENELOPE. But why is it out of bounds? For what reason?

CLIVE *(shaking his head)*. My sweet, in the army there is never any reason for anything. I suppose one of the Brass Hats thought it would be rather a good idea, what!

PENELOPE. It's a shame! Just think! *(Turning to him.)* We could have run over there, had a meal, seen the show . . . had another meal and come back on the last bus.

CLIVE. Darling, you must be hungry. It sounds marvelous, but as you English say, "We've 'ad it." Mind if I smoke?

PENELOPE *(indicating the cigarette-box)*. Of course. Plenty there. Help yourself.

(CLIVE *gets a cigarette.* IDA *appears at the door,* L.)

IDA. 'Scuse me!

PENELOPE *(surprised)*. Oh, Ida! Haven't you gone yet?

IDA. Yes'm. I've been and come back.

PENELOPE. Why? Have you forgotten something?

IDA. Yes'm. Mr. Toopses' trousers.

PENELOPE. What?

IDA. You know'm. You said you wanted Mother to put a patch on the . . .

PENELOPE. Oh yes, I remember. I brought the whole suit down this morning. *(She crosses to the closet* L., *and produces a black suit on a hanger.)* Here you are. Ask your mother to look to the jacket cuffs and . . .

IDA *(taking the suit.)* Ow'm! This isn't it!

PENELOPE *(who has moved to* C.*)* Not?

IDA. No'm! This is Mr. Toopses' second-best suit.

CLIVE (L. *of the settee*). How many suits has he got?

PENELOPE. Three.

CLIVE. Black market!

PENELOPE. Oh, damn! Then where have I put the other?

IDA (*crossing to and ascending staircase.*) I'd better go and look for it.

PENELOPE. Yes. No! Wait a moment. I'll go. I think I know just where to lay my hands on it. (IDA *comes down the stairs again.*) Sorry, Clive. (*Going upstairs.*) Won't be a minute. (*She exits upstairs.*)

IDA (*after a pause*). Turned out nice again, 'asn't it?

CLIVE. Not 'arf! (*Staring.*) Eh? Oh—er—yes. Yes, rather. (*He turns away* R. *and giggles.*)

(*A slight pause.*)

IDA. I'm Ida.

CLIVE (*turning*). I beg your pardon?

IDA. I'm Ida.

CLIVE. Oh, I'm so sorry.

IDA. No, I'm IDA!

CLIVE (*trying not to laugh*). Oh yes!—You're Ida —— Oh, I'm awfully glad about that.

IDA. Don't mention it.

CLIVE (*pulling her leg*). Do you know who *I* am?

IDA (*agog*). No?

CLIVE (*shaking his head solemnly*). Eisenhower's the name.

IDA. Go on, you're pulling my leg.

CLIVE. As if I would.

IDA. Well, I think you're 'eaven!

CLIVE. Oh, that's beautiful. Ida, we must go to the pictures together some night.

IDA (*delighted*). Ow! But I won't have another night off till next Wednesday.

CLIVE. Never mind—Heaven can wait.

(PENELOPE *re-enters downstairs with another dark suit.)*

PENELOPE *(coming down and giving* IDA *the suit and taking the other one from her).* Here you are, Ida. Ask your mother to do the best she can with it.

IDA. Don't you worry'm. Mother'll make it so as you won't know it.

PENELOPE *(to* C.) Will she make it so that Mr. Toop can *wear* it? That's all I ask.

IDA. I shouldn't wonder'm. I'll fetch it back with me to-night and put it upstairs and I'd better put this one *(the second-best suit)* away'm?

PENELOPE *(wanting her to go).* No, don't bother. I'll do that. Have you brown paper and string in the kitchen?

IDA. I think so.

PENELOPE *(shoo-ing her out of the room).* Well—er—run along.

IDA. I wish you were in these!

(She smiles knowingly at PENELOPE: *turns to* CLIVE, *giggles, and rushes out down* L.)

PENELOPE. You have made a hit.

CLIVE. Dainty morsel, that!

PENELOPE. Ida? She's an absolute joy. I wouldn't be without her for the world.

CLIVE. Oh, well. "One man's pyjamas is another man's night-shirt." You can't get away from that.

PENELOPE. Never mind about Ida. Listen, Clive, I've got an idea! Turn round.

CLIVE *(protesting).* Look here . . .

PENELOPE. Will you . . . *(She spins him round and looks him up and down.)*

CLIVE. What *is* this? Medical inspection? Ninety-nine. *(He coughs.)*

PENELOPE. Near enough for size—— You can wear this!

CLIVE. What?

PENELOPE. Lionel's other suit.

CLIVE. *What?* Me a parson? Don't be silly, darling! I'd be court martialed!

PENELOPE. Why not? If you go as a civilian, who's to know you're a soldier?

CLIVE *(not liking the idea)*. Yes, but . . .

PENELOPE. "Private Lives," Clive. A dinner and a lovely drink, Clive.

CLIVE. Oh, all right, but don't forget I have to get into uniform before I go back to camp. *(Starts undressing)*.

PENELOPE. What time are you due back?

CLIVE. Any time before midnight.

PENELOPE. And we shall be back shortly after ten. That gives you plenty of time to change again.

CLIVE. But won't your husband object? I'd kick up a big fuss myself.

PENELOPE. So will he when it's too late to do anything about it, but we shall be back long before he is, so he need never know.

CLIVE *(catching at straws)*. But suppose . . .

PENELOPE. Suppose nothing. If anyone asks any questions, just say your name is Humphrey.

CLIVE. But why Humphrey?

PENELOPE. Oh, he's just a man who's coming to take the service to-morrow.

CLIVE. But—I——

PENELOPE. Take these things in there *(pointing R. to the dining-room)* and change.

CLIVE. Wait a minute. Let me learn my part. My name is Humphrey, and I'm just a man who's coming over to take the service to-morrow. I shan't really have to take the service, shall I?

PENELOPE. No, of course not.

CLIVE. Why must I go in there?

PENELOPE. For the simple season that *I* shall be in here.

CLIVE *(taking the suit and going into the dining-*

room). Oh! I see what you mean. But I wish it to be put on record that I don't like it. I've played in too many plays where characters have done this sort of thing, and something's always gone wrong.

PENELOPE. Yes, darling; but it's always righted itself by the last act. Go on—get changed. Leave the door open, then I can talk to you.

CLIVE. I still don't like it.

PENELOPE *(going to the door* L.*)* Ida!

CLIVE. Don't bring her in here!

PENELOPE. I'm not. I was just making sure she's gone!

(PENELOPE *crosses to the closet* L. *and brings out a clerical hat and collar, which she puts on the sofa. She sings snatches of "Some Day I'll find You" from "Private Lives.")*

CLIVE *(speaking off stage).* That brings back memories.

PENELOPE. You mean the song?

CLIVE. Yes. Every night, all through the tour, the suspense of wondering if you'd manage to start on the right note.

PENELOPE *(protesting).* Clive! *(She goes up* C.*)*

CLIVE. Followed by the agony of knowing that you hadn't!

PENELOPE *(crossing to the door* R.*)* I *beg* your pardon? *(Moving quickly away.)* Oh, I beg your pardon! *(She goes down below the sofa).*

(CLIVE *re-enters* R. *He is wearing the trousers of the suit, and carrying the jacket and waistcoat, and also the uniform.)*

CLIVE. *(to* C.*)* It's all right, you're too late. I say, what do I do about a collar? *(He puts the clothes on the back of the sofa.)*

PENELOPE. You can wear one of Lionel's.

CLIVE. "Dog" or otherwise?

PENELOPE. "Dog."

CLIVE Oh no! Oh no! I refuse—flatly refuse. I will not add sacrilege to my other crimes.

PENELOPE (*holding up clerical collar*—CLIVE *winces*). Turn round! (*Climbing on the settee.*)

CLIVE. What, again?

(*He turns.* PENELOPE *puts the collar round his neck.*)

PENELOPE. And keep still or I'll choke you!

CLIVE. What do you think you're doing now? (*As* PENELOPE *tugs and heaves, trying to make the collar meet.*) Hi! Steady! My name isn't Skillon.

PENELOPE. At this moment I wish it were.

CLIVE What is the size of this collar?

PENELOPE. Just fifteen.

CLIVE. "Just fifteen." And I take just sixteen! (*Heavenly.*) Still what is an inch amongst friends? Do me a favor . . . Swallow, I can't.

PENELOPE (*having fastened the collar*—*panting*). There! (*picking up the uniform.*) Now we've got to put this somewhere where it won't be found. (*She crosses to* C.)

CLIVE (*putting on the clerical jacket*). *And* where it can be found when we get back.

PENELOPE (*looking round and finally seeing the chest* R. *of the stairs*). This will do. Nobody ever goes into the chest. Nothing in it but tennis rackets and Lionel's golf clubs. (*She puts the uniform in the chest.*)

CLIVE (*now fully dressed. Surveying himself, ruefully*). Of course, I look like a fountain-pen. (*He puts on the clerical hat, but after glancing in the mirror* R., *he removes it quickly.*) What do I do with the bib thing?

PENELOPE (*crossing to him, below the settee*). It goes inside, silly. (*She adjusts it.*) Oh, Clive, I am looking forward to this! I wonder if the girl who plays Amanda gets as many laughs as I did.

CLIVE. I wonder if the man who plays Elyot gets as many bruises as I used to.

PENELOPE. What do you mean by that?

CLIVE. You know very well what I mean. The fight at the end of Act Two.

PENELOPE. What about it?

CLIVE. My God! Have you forgotten how you used to lose your head completely and nearly strangle me?

PENELOPE. I did not!

CLIVE. And that final blow that was supposed to knock me off my feet. Never once did you get that blow in at the right moment!

PENELOPE. That is a *deliberate* lie.

CLIVE. Never once.

PENELOPE *(almost in tears)*. Clive!

CLIVE. Oh, I beg your pardon. ONCE.

PENELOPE. Thank you.

CLIVE *(mournfully)*. The last night of the tour? (PENELOPE *strides away up* L.C., *and back.)* It was so simple. I remember just how it was supposed to go. Your last line was "Beast: brute: swine: devil:" and you were supposed to hit me on the "devil."

PENELOPE. Well?

CLIVE. Instead of which I invariably got it—when I was quite unprepared for it—on the "swine."

PENELOPE *(crosses to him)*. Because you *would* move away from me. If I hadn't got it in then, I should have had to canter right across the stage to catch you.

CLIVE. My dear girl. . . . *(Desperately.)* Look . . . I was on the floor . . . you were on top of me . . .

PENELOPE. I remember that, over and over again.

CLIVE. Listen, can you remember the lines?

PENELOPE. Can I ever forget them?

CLIVE. Then I'll show you what I mean. Go on from your line "This is the end"—you remember?

PENELOPE. Yes. *(She moves to position.)* I was here. (CLIVE *takes position.)* Ready?   *(WARN Curtain.)*

CLIVE. Fire away.

PENELOPE *(as* AMANDA, *very quietly)*. "This is the

end, do you understand? The end, finally and forever."
*(She moves to (imaginary) door and makes gesture of
wrenching it open.* CLIVE *(as* ELYOT) *rushes after her
and clutches her wrists.)*

CLIVE (ELYOT). "You're not going like this."

PENELOPE (AMANDA). "Oh, yes, I am."

CLIVE (ELYOT). "You're not."

PENELOPE (AMANDA). "I am, let go of me——
*(He pulls her away from the "door" and they struggle.
Breathlessly as they fight.)* "You're a cruel fiend, and
I hate and loathe you; thank God I've realized in time
what you're really like; marry you again, never, never,
never . . . I'd rather die in torment . . ."

CLIVE *(as* ELYOT: *at the same time).* "Shut up; shut
up; I wouldn't marry you again if you came crawling to
me on your bended knees; you're a mean, evil-minded
little vampire—I hope to God I never set eyes on you
again as long as I live . . ."

*(At this point of the proceedings they trip over a piece
of carpet down* C., *and fall to the floor, rolling over
and over in paroxysms of rage. As they fall on the
floor* MISS SKILLON *appears at the French windows.
She cannot at first see* CLIVE *and* PENELOPE *rolling
on the floor.)*

MISS SKILLON *(as she enters).* . . . I . . . *(When she
gets down stage she sees the struggling forms on the
ground. She does not get a clear view of* CLIVE'S *face,
so mistakes him for* LIONEL. *Horrified.)* Oh, Mrs.
Toop! Mr. Toop! ! ! ! *(*PENELOPE *and* CLIVE *are by
this time lost to all but the scene they are enacting. Fluttering round.)* Mr. Toop, I beg of you. Do desist. I
don't blame you, in a way, but really . . . *(She continues
to protest. Finally* PENELOPE (AMANDA) *breaks free
and half gets up.* CLIVE (ELYOT) *grabs her leg and she
falls, if possible, against a table, knocking it over. Protesting.)* Oh! This is too dreadful *and* the Harvest

Festival to-morrow! Mrs. Toop! *(She moves close to* PENELOPE.)

PENELOPE (AMANDA) *(screaming)*. "BEAST: BRUTE; SWINE; DEVIL!"

(And on the "devil" she lands out with what is intended to be a stinging blow for CLIVE. *Unfortunately she misses him, and catches* MISS SKILLON *full in the face.* MISS SKILLON *sinks to the floor unconscious.)*

QUICK CURTAIN

ACT TWO

SCENE.—*The same*

TIME.—*The same day—10 p. m.*

When the CURTAIN *rises, the stage is in darkness, except for the moonlight, which streams in through the French windows.*

*After a pause—*LIONEL'S *voice is heard off—down L.*

CHOIRBOY (*off*). Are you sure you can manage, Mr. Toop?

LIONEL (*off*). Yes, thank you. I can manage perfectly well. Thank you. *Good* night, Willie.

CHOIRBOY (*off*). Good night, Mr. Toop.

(Then the door down L. opens and LIONEL *comes slowly and carefully into the room. He carries in his arms two bottles—one whiskey and one brandy.)*

LIONEL (*surprised on finding the room in darkness*). Oh! (*With a great deal of fumbling and clinking he puts the bottles on a table. To himself, as he takes off his hat and coat.*) Extraordinary! (*Calling.*) Penelope! (*Putting his hat and coat in the closet.*) PENELOPE!!

*(A sleepy, quavering, female voice (*MISS SKILLON'S*) is heard singing, slowly.)*

MISS SKILLON. "We plough the fields and scat. . ."

(The top note changes into a wail of agony.)

LIONEL (*alarmed*). What was that? (*As he comes*

33

from the closet.) Penelope, is that you? Where are you? *(He switches on the lights at the door down L. and crosses towards the sofa, then stops dead at C. MISS SKILLON is laid out, full length on the sofa, one arm hangs loosely down and in her hand is an empty tumbler, and by her side an almost empty sherry bottle. Mystified.)* Miss Skillon ! !

MISS SKILLON *(opening one eye, and murmuring vaguely).*

> "And with him sporting on the green,
>   His little grandchild,
>   Wilhelmine."

LIONEL *(horrified).* Good heavens. Miss Skillon, what *has* happened to you?

MISS SKILLON *(still burbling).* "I'm a better man than you are, Gunga Din."

LIONEL *(shrugging his shoulders helplessly, picking up the bottle from the floor. Holding it to the light).* Empty—almost. *(He takes the glass from MISS SKILLON's hand and puts it with the bottle on the table.)* Miss Skillon! *(Shaking her gently.)* Miss Skillon, do you feel—er—*well* enough to sit up?

MISS SKILLON. Sit up? Who with?

LIONEL *(imploringly).* Please! You must pull yourself together. How on earth did you get here—in this —er—condition?

MISS SKILLON. My—legs. What's the matter with my legs?

LIONEL. Your legs?

MISS SKILLON. My legs. They lack co-ordination!

LIONEL *(gingerly, taking her ankles).* Perhaps if I . . .

MISS SKILLON *(giggling).* Cave man! (LIONEL *assists her to a sitting position.)* Why, it's Mr. Toop!

LIONEL. Yes. Do you feel better?

MISS SKILLON. Better than what?

LIONEL. Miss Skillon, you really must get a grip on yourself.

MISS SKILLON. That woman! She struck me!

LIONEL. What? What woman? *(Sitting on her L.)* Miss Skillon, what has happened here to-night?

MISS SKILLON *(firmly)*. Nothing! *(Taking his hand.)* It shall be *our* little secret.

LIONEL. Our little secret?

MISS SKILLON. When I saw what the woman was doing to you ... !

LIONEL. To me? What woman?

MISS SKILLON. My heart bled for you. *(LIONEL clutches his head in desperation.)* No wonder she wears trousers!

LIONEL *(to himself)*. Inebriated! Hopelessly!

MISS SKILLON *(singing)*. "—oh mares eat oats and does eat oats and little lambs eat ivy!" *(LIONEL rises, leaves MISS SKILLON, and looks round helplessly, then crosses to the table down R., opens a drawer and produces a large bottle of smelling-salts. He advances toward MISS SKILLON. Vaguely.)* What's that?

LIONEL *(holding the bottle at arm's length and shoving it under MISS SKILLON's nose)*. Smell ! !

MISS SKILLON *(after a quick and noisy intake of breath)*. OH ! ! California, here I come! *(And she falls back flat on the settee.)*

LIONEL *(fluttering around—alarmed)*. Oh! What have I done? Miss Skillon! *(Slapping her hand.)* Miss Skillon ! ! *(He looks round wildly—sees the bottles he brought in and crosses to them, murmuring.)* Brandy! *(He picks up the brandy bottle, removes the capsule, pours some into a glass, returns to MISS SKILLON, kneels beside her on the settee, one arm round her, and holds the glass to her lips.)* Sit up and drink this.

(LIONEL is in this position when IDA wanders in from down L. IDA comes down stage L.C., stops and looks aghast. LIONEL turns his head and sees her. MISS SKILLON lolls back.)

IDA. WELL! Don't mind me!

(She exits hastily.)

LIONEL. Ida! Come here! Ida! ! (IDA *returns.*) Ida, Miss Skillon is not well.

IDA. Why, what's happened?

LIONEL. I don't know. I came in here just now and found Miss Skillon . . . found her . . . well—*found her.*

IDA. Oh yeah!

LIONEL. Ida, do you know how Miss Skillon came to be here?

IDA *(at the door)*. I shall say what *I* have to say in the witness-box! *(She sweeps out.)*

LIONEL *(blank amazement)*. In the witness-box? . . . What on earth . . . ? *(He calls.)* IDA! *(But answer comes there none. The telephone rings. Jumping up.)* Oh, my goodness! *(Rushing round to the 'phone.)* Hullo? Hullo? . . . Yes . . . The Vicar speaking . . . Who? . . . THE POLICE! ! . . . Oh, my goodness! . . . Yes? Oh yes, Sergeant? . . . A what? . . . A Russian spy? Escaped from the guard house at the Air Base? Yes, of course . . . one cannot be too careful . . . er . . . is he armed? . . . Oh! Then I shall most *certainly* take every precaution. Thank you, Sergeant, thank you. Good night! Goood night ! ! *(He replaces the reeciver, and, wiping his brow, wanders to c.)* Oh dear! What with one thing *(looking at MISS SKILLON)* and another . . . *(He crosses to MISS SKILLON and shakes her gingerly.)* Miss Skillon! *(MISS SKILLON opens her eyes and sits up.)* Miss Skillon, wouldn't you like to go home?

MISS SKILLON. Who with?

LIONEL. Oh dear! *(He crosses down R., rings servant bell—then returns to R. of MISS SKILLON.)* I do not wish to alarm you, but there's a dangerous character abroad to-night.

MISS SKILLON. Bring him here! I feel like a lion that has tasted blood!

(Enter IDA L.)

IDA. Did you ring?

LIONEL *(crossing to* C.*)*. Ida, please answer my questions. Do you know where Mrs. Toop has gone?

IDA. Not a word will I breathe. You can't make me an accelerator before the fact.

MISS SKILLON *(vaguely)*. Over and over! I saw it happening, before my very eyes.

LIONEL *(turning to her)*. What did you see, Miss Skillon?

MISS SKILLON. Over and over. With my own eyes I saw them. "Sweetheart" he called her.

LIONEL. I cannot make head or tail of all this. Ida, has someone been here to see Mrs. Toop?

IDA. My lips are sealed!

MISS SKILLON. Over and over! With my own eyes I saw it.

LIONEL. Yes, so you keep saying, Miss Skillon. But you don't say *what* you saw.

MISS SKILLON. Mr. Toop, if you have forgotten, then so have I. It is a closed book. *(She leans back and closes her eyes.)*

(LIONEL *turns to* IDA.*)*

LIONEL. It's no use, Ida, Miss Skillon will have to stay the night.

IDA. WHAT??

LIONEL. Miss Skillon is not well.

IDA. She's squiffy!

LIONEL. Ida! !

IDA. Tight as an owl?

LIONEL. Don't glare at me, girl, in that offensive manner. I am not responsible for Miss Skillon's—er—condition.

IDA. Then 'ow did she get hold of the cooking-sherry?

LIONEL. Will you kindly stop asking stupid questions and go and prepare a bed for Miss Skillon?

IDA. I'll get some 'ot-water bottles. *(She goes to the door* L.*)*

LIONEL. Hurry back and help me get Miss Skillon upstairs. (IDA *exits.*) Where can Pepenope be? *(Wandering round the room, distressed, suddenly crossing to the telephone and dialing: after a pause.)* Hullo? . . . Hullo? . . . Is that the Grange? Oh, is that you, Mrs. Chittenden-Cholmondley? The Vicar speaking. I was wondering if my wife had called on you this evening— you see, a prisoner has escaped from the guard house. Yes . . . Armed too . . . Well, thank you so much, Mrs. Chittenden-Cholmondley . . . so sorry to have troubled you. Good night. Goood night. *(He replaces the receiver and comes down C. There is a slight bumping noise from direction of the dining-room—*LIONEL *jumps.)* What was that? *(He crosses up R. to the dining-room door and opens it gingerly.)* Er—anyone there? *(He is afraid to go in . . . looks round . . . then goes up to the windows and fastens them. As he is doing this* IDA *enters down L.)*

IDA *(ominously).* Goin' out?

LIONEL *(jumping).* Oh! Oh, it's only you! No, I am fastening this window. It should not have been left unlocked. *(Coming down C.)* Ida, where is my hockeystick?

IDA *(laconically).* That won't bring her round.

LIONEL. I did not ask for your crude observations, girl. I asked you where my hockey-stick is.

IDA. It's in the chest there. *(Pointing.)* Where it's always been.

LIONEL *(crossing to the chest).* Any more of your rudeness, Ida, and I'm afraid we shall have to part company.

IDA. Don't worry. After what I've seen to-night, I'm parting!

LIONEL *(opening the chest).* Good heavens! *(He produces* CLIVE'S *uniform.)* Ida! How did these get in here?

(He comes down R. of the table. IDA *moves in to L.C.,*

taking the uniform. She sees the stripe on a sleeve, and starts.)

IDA. They ain't mine!

LIONEL. I am perfectly well aware of that fact. *(Suddenly.)* Good heavens! *(Frightened.)* Ida, did you lock the back door when you came in?

IDA. No, but I meant to.

LIONEL. Go and lock it at once.

IDA. But . . .

LIONEL *(barking at her)*. Don't stand there gaping! Do as I tell you! Lock the back door and come back here at once. I want to speak to you. (IDA *goes down* L.) I'm afraid something terrible has happened in this house to-night!

IDA *(turning at the door)*. So your conscience is pricking you at last. *(She exits with the uniform.)*

LIONEL *(very agitated)*. Wretched girl! *(Crosses to the telephone, and lifts the receiver.)* The police . . . I wonder . . . should I . . . Yes! Hello! Hello!

(In the meantime a MAN *clad in blue denim dungarees and coat enters up* R. *Back of coat lettered with large "P". LIONEL turns and sees him.)*

LIONEL. Hello! I mean—er—who are you? What do you want?

MAN. I want your clothes.

LIONEL. My clothes?

MAN. *(Giving Red salute—clenched fist with bent elbow, the poker in his hand pointing* R.) Tovarisch! *(Pronounced: Tuh-VAH-rich).*

LIONEL. *(Looking where poker points)* Where?

*(*MAN *hits him on head with poker. LIONEL collapses in his arms.* MAN *drags him into dining-room. IDA re-enters down* L.)

IDA *(as she enters)*. I've locked it! Oh! *(She looks*

round mystified—calls.) Mr. Toop! *(Pregnant silence.)*
Mr. Toop! *(She sees the telephone receiver hanging
loose.)* 'Ere! What's going on 'ere! *(She calls again.)*
Mr. Toop! ! *(Picking up the receiver from the floor.)*
Hello! Hello!

MISS SKILLON. Hello!

IDA *(jumping).* Ow. *(Then.)* Oh, it's only you,
pickled herring.

MISS SKILLON *(sitting up).* Where am I?

IDA *(replacing the receiver).* You're where you've no
right to be.

MISS SKILLON. What has happened?

IDA. That's what I'd like to know. Did you see where
he went?

MISS SKILLON. See—see who?

IDA. 'Im, Mr. Toop.

MISS SKILLON. Yes, I saw. What a rough and
tumble! Dreadful!

IDA. You an' Mr. Toop, an' you ought to be ashamed
of yourselves.

MISS SKILLON. Ida, what have I done?

IDA. Who can tell?

MISS SKILLON. Ida, if this ever becomes known in
the village, I'm a ruined woman. Never have I touched
a drop of alcohol in my life before.

IDA. Well, you've certainly made up for it to-night.
(There is a ring at the front DOORBELL.) Ow! Who
ever's that?

MISS SKILLON. Ida, I musn't be seen here! *(Rises.)*
Not like this.

IDA. Can you walk?

MISS SKILLON. Of course I can walk. *(She tries to
rise.)* The spirit is willing.

IDA. But the legs ain't. 'Ere, you'd better come upstairs. *(The BELL rings again.)* Ow, wait a minute,
can't you? *(Looking around.)* 'Ere! Now you stop
there. *(Propping MISS SKILLON against the newelpost
at the foot of the stairs.)* An' not a word do you utter!
(She moves to the door and then rushes back just in

time to catch MISS SKILLON *as she topples forward. The BELL rings again. She props* MISS SKILLON *up.)*
I'm coming! I'm coming! *(She exits down* L.)

MISS SKILLON *(left alone).* Now what has she left me here for? *(She turns her head to see* LIONEL *enter up* R. *His trousers have been removed, but he still wears his clerical jacket.)* Oh! Mr. Toop! Mr. Toop! *(She exits hastily into the closet* L.)

(The MAN *enters* R. *He gives a fresh blow on the head to* LIONEL, *who again collapses into his arms, and is dragged off into the dining-room* R.)

BISHOP *(off stage* L.). Mrs. Toop is expecting me.

(Re-enter IDA. *She holds the door open and curtseys.)*

IDA *(with much awe).* This way, your Highness! *(The* BISHOP OF LAX *enters* L. *carrying a suitcase. He wears an overcoat over his bishop's garb. He is a large, jovial-looking man. He crosses* R. *Closing the door and looking for* MISS SKILLON.) Now where's she gone? *(She moves up* L.C., *looking around.)*

BISHOP *(misunderstanding).* Did she say when she would be back?

IDA *(continuing her search).* She never said she was goin'.

BISHOP. And I suppose Mr. Toop is with her?

IDA *(uneasily).* Shall I take your things, your Highness?

BISHOP. My things? Oh, yes. Thank you. *(He hands her his hat and suitcase.)*

IDA *(nervously, as she deposits the suitcase near the foot of the stairs).* Turned out nice again, 'asn't it? *(She returns to* R.C.)

BISHOP. Er—yes. I suppose it has. *(Removing his overcoat.)*

IDA. We wasn't expecting you till to-morrow. *(Taking the overcoat.)*

BISHOP. I suppose there will be a bed for me somewhere.

IDA *(muttering)*. Yes, somewhere, some'ow. *(She
goes vaguely up stage and then starts to climb the stairs,
carrying the BISHOP's coat and hat.)*

BISHOP *(curiously)*. Who are you?

IDA. I'm Ida. *(At the top of the stairs, peering round
the corner, still in search of MISS SKILLON.)*

BISHOP. "Ida"! Oh, well, of course that explains
everything, doesn't it?

IDA *(turning to look across at him)*. Eh?

BISHOP *(patiently)*. Just what are you doing here?

IDA. Well, I'm *Ida!* I'm the maid.

BISHOP *(seeing light)*. Oh, the maid!

IDA *(coming down stairs, brightly)*. Of course you
wouldn't never think it, seeing me all dressed up like
this, would you? *(The BISHOP gapes at her. At c.)* Mind
you, your Highness, if I'd known it was you at the
front door, I'd have slipped into my uniform, even
though it was my night out.

BISHOP *(with a wave of the hand meaning "Go")*.
You are forgiven.

IDA. Well, sit down, your Highness, and I'll get you
some supper.

BISHOP. I want nothing to eat, thank you.

IDA *(shouting)*. Sit down, anyway. *(The BISHOP sits
hastily on sofa)*. 'Scuse me, but I'm a bit put out to-
night.

BISHOP *(doubtfully)*. You're quite well, aren't you?

IDA. Oh, yes, ever so! *(Holding out the hat and
coat, etc.)* I'll—I'll just get rid of these.

*(She moves to the closet L., and opens the door, hurling
the things in wildly. There is a low groan from MISS
SKILLON in the closet. IDA slams the door to, and
turns facing the BISHOP, who, hearing the groan,
jumps up.)*

BISHOP. What was that?

IDA. What?

BISHOP. I thought I heard someone groan.

IDA *(hastily)*. That was me—leastways, it was my neuritis.

BISHOP *(sitting)*. Neuritis. You have my sympathy. I get a touch of it now and again. Mine is in the arm.

IDA. Mine's in the closet. *(She exits down L., in a hurry.)*

BISHOP *(to himself)*. I suppose every village has one! *(He sees the bottles on the table, crosses to L.C., picks up the brandy bottle, holds it up, then looks in the direction of the departed IDA. LIONEL appears up R., clad in undershirt, shoes, socks and with table-cloth tied around his bare legs. He is dazed and carries a poker. He starts toward the BISHOP who turns and sees him. Putting down the bottle—amazed.)* Good Heavens!

LIONEL *(raising the poker: in a dull voice)*. To-varisch! *(The BISHOP, with a loud cry, dodges and rushes across to behind the R. end of the sofa, where he gets down on the floor, and cannot see LIONEL, who mechanically brings the poker down as if on a head. He then begins to chant in a low voice:)* Moscow calling! Moscow calling!

(While doing this he wanders absently over to the closet door, opens it, enters and closes the door after him. The BISHOP comes from his hiding-place. He wipes his brow as he looks round, making sure he is alone. He is very shaken. He crosses to R. of the table and picks up bottle as IDA enters down L.)

IDA *(brightly—seeing the BISHOP with the bottle)*. That's right, your Highness, make yourself at 'ome.

(She begins to ascend the staircase. She has a hot-water bottle in each hand.)

BISHOP *(tremulously)*. Here, young woman, come here. *(He drinks the brandy and moves to C., as IDA comes downstairs to* L. *of him.)* Have you a brother in this house?

IDA. I 'aven't no brother at all. Why?

BISHOP. A lunatic came in here a moment ago.

IDA. WHAT??

BISHOP. He attacked me with a rod of iron.

IDA *(after a look at the brandy, with meaning).* I'll fetch the soda-water. *(She crosses to the door* L.)

BISHOP *(testily).* I don't want any soda-water. I want to know who it was that attacked me just now.

IDA *(at the door).* P'r'aps it was a mirage! *(She crosses to the table* L.C., *puts down the hot-water bottles and comes to* L. *of the* BISHOP, C.)

BISHOP. A what?

IDA. A mirage. I've just been reading about them in my "weekly." In one story, the 'ero—Digby 'is name is—is searching for 'is manhood. *(A quick look from the* BISHOP.) After many weeks 'is search 'as taken 'im into the burning desert, an he's dying of thirst. His throat is as raw as a red-'ot cinder, 'is swollen, blackened tongue is lolling out of 'is mouth and talon fingers is clawin' at 'is vitals . . .

BISHOP *(quietly).* I think I'm going to be sick! I tell you a man clad in his underwear came in here and threatened me with a rod of iron. *(Crossing* R.C. *to below the settee.)*

IDA. And where did he go?

BISHOP *(hesitantly).* I—er—I didn't notice.

IDA *(placing both hands on his shoulders and pushing him down into the sofa.)* Yes, well, you sit down, your 'Ighness, and take it easy.

(The door down L. *opens and* PENELOPE *enters. On seeing the* BISHOP *she dashes back to the door, but it is too late.)*

BISHOP *(rising).* Penelope, my dear!

*(*IDA *moves to* C., *and is about to speak.)*

PENELOPE *(as she crosses to him and embraces him.)*
Uncle! This is a surprise. Sit down, my dear. You said
you weren't coming until to-morrow.

(IDA *moves down* R. *of* PENELOPE *and tries to attract
her attention by tapping her elbow.* PENELOPE *ab-
stractedly scratches her elbow and ignores* IDA.)

BISHOP I know, my dear, but that hotel! Too awful
for words. I just packed my things after dinner and
fled.

(IDA *and* PENELOPE *repeat the elbow business.)*

PENELOPE. T-t-t! And you've been here all alone.
BISHOP *(looking towards* IDA). No, not alone!
PENELOPE *(turning and following his look.)* Oh, you
mean Ida. It's all right, Ida. You can go to bed. I'll
look after the Bishop.
IDA *(anxiously).* Can I 'ave a word with you'm alone?
PENELOPE What? No, not now, Ida. In the morning.
IDA. But you don't know what's happened'm!
BISHOP. Don't worry yourself. I'll tell Mrs. Toop.
IDA. But I don't mean what you mean. Miss Skillon'm.
PENELOPE. Never mind about Miss Skillon now, Ida.
Just put those bottles in the Bishop's bed. (IDA *picks
up the brandy and whiskey bottles from the table, and
commences ascending the stairs.)* Not those bottles,
Ida, the hot-water bottles! (IDA *descends the stairs,
crosses to the table* L.C., *and puts down the bottles, picking up the hot-water bottles.)* Ida, come here—let me
feel those bottles. (IDA *crosses to her,* C. *Feeling the
bottles.)* Just as I thought! They're stone cold! Go and
fill them again. And use *hot* water this time. (IDA *tries
to attract* PENELOPE's *attention with strange waving of
the arms.)* What *is* the matter with you, Ida?
BISHOP. Alcohol, my dear.
IDA *(in despair).* Shall I put your coat away'm? *(She
tugs* PENELOPE's *sleeve.)*

PENELOPE. No, thank you. I can do that myself. All I ask you to do is fill those bottles again.

IDA. Well, I've done my best. *(She exits down L., still making signs.)*

(CLIVE is off, singing: "Some Day I'll Find You." PENELOPE is nervous and distrait. She looks anxiously towards the door down L. and moves furtively towards it.)

BISHOP *(just as PENELOPE reaches the door)*. Well, my dear . .

PENELOPE *(startled)*. Well, Uncle, it is nice to see you again. Have you been here long?

(CLIVE is still singing.)

BISHOP. What is that noise?

PENELOPE *(quickly)*. That? Oh, that's the radio. I'll go and switch it off.

(She flies off down L. There is a BANG off-stage and a yell of agony from CLIVE. The BISHOP rises, gapes after her in astonishment, then turns R., as IDA re-enters.)

IDA *(as she enters.)* Please'm! *(The BISHOP spins round. Seeing the BISHOP alone.)* Oh! Where's she got to now?

(She exits again quickly. The BISHOP sits, facing down stage, bewildered. The MAN, in LIONEL'S clothes, carrying his own denims, enters from the dining-room up R. He sees the BISHOP on the sofa, goes out through the windows, opening them rather noisily. The BISHOP jumps up, looks around, moves up stage and closes windows. PENELOPE re-enters. The BISHOP moves down R.C.)

PENELOPE *(too brightly).* Well! Well! Well! Darling, you must be tired. Why don't you go to bed? *(Tugging at the* BISHOP's *arm as he attempts to reseat himself on the sofa.)*

BISHOP. I do not want to go to bed. *(Below the sofa.)* Penelope, what is the mystery?

PENELOPE *(L. of the sofa).* Mystery, Uncle?

BISHOP. It's no use you standing there acting yourself silly. I want to know what is wrong.

PENELOPE. I don't know *what* you are talking about, darling.

BISHOP. You don't, eh? Then why are you behaving so queerly? What is the matter with that maid of yours? And *who* was the lunatic that attacked me just now?

PENELOPE. WHAT??

BISHOP. I'm not going to say all that again. I will merely tell you that a lunatic—a wild-eyed creature in a state of—er—undress, appeared from nowhere and threatened me with a poker.

PENELOPE. Uncle!

BISHOP. He disappeared as mysteriously as he came. When I questioned your maid, she—very clumsily, I thought—denied all knowledge of him.

PENELOPE. Well, sit down again, darling. I'll put my coat away, then we'll talk it over quietly. *(She takes off her coat and moves to the closet.)*

BISHOP *(sitting on the sofa and facing front).* Penelope, will you please stop trying to "humor" me. I assure you I am in complete possession of all my faculties—and—forgive my saying so—I am beginning to think I am the only person in the house who is. (PENELOPE, *in the meantime, has opened the closet door. As she puts her coat in, a little gasp comes from her and a look of horror on to her face. She puts her hand over her mouth to prevent herself from screaming, closes the door and falls to the floor in a faint. Meanwhile the* BISHOP *is rambling on ponderously.)* I tell you again, I have been attacked by a lunatic. He came in here, almost naked, brandishing a rod of iron. *(He turns, can-*

not see PENELOPE *who is hidden by the table, and says irritably:)* Now where . . . ? Penelope! *(He rises and crosses L.)* Pen—— *(He sees* PENELOPE *on the floor.)* Merciful heavens! *(Bending over her.)* Are you dead? This is dreadful! *(A low moan comes from* PENELOPE.) Oh! Just a faint! Air! Air! Where is that half-witted maid? *(He goes to the door down L.—opens it, and* CLIVE, *who has obviously been on hands and knees peeping through the keyhole, falls into the room. Starting.)* What on earth!!! Good heavens! *(CLIVE, on the floor, is nonplussed. He first attempts to salute, and then, still on his knees, places his palms together in what he imagines is a devout manner.)* What are you doing there?

CLIVE. Praying.

BISHOP. Oh!! *(He stands back from the door, revealing* PENELOPE *to* CLIVE.)

CLIVE *(still on the floor)*. What are you doing with Penelope?

BISHOP. She fainted.

CLIVE. Why?

BISHOP *(testily)*. How the—— How should I know? Does she often faint?

CLIVE. How the—— How should I know?

BISHOP. Well, really! Don't supplicate there, man! Help me to put her on the sofa. *(CLIVE rises and takes* PENELOPE'S *legs. The* BISHOP *takes her head.)* Carefully! Don't joggle her! *(They place her on the sofa with her head to the L. end.)* Now I'll get some brandy. *(He crosses to the table L.C.)*

CLIVE (C., R. *of the* BISHOP). I can't understand this at all. She was perfectly all right when she left me a few minutes ago. It must have been the shock of seeing you.

BISHOP. *What??*

CLIVE. It caught *me* below the belt, I can tell you!

BISHOP *(holding out brandy)*. Here! You give it to her. It will be best if her eyes fall on you first when she comes round.

CLIVE *(taking the glass)*. Why?

BISHOP. It will give her confidence.

CLIVE. I doubt it. Come along, darling. Have a little dinkey-winkey. She'll be all right in a moment. *(As he turns away to say this to the* BISHOP, PENELOPE's *head rolls over so that he replaces the glass in the wrong place.)* Come along, darling . . . I say, have you got a straw or something?

BISHOP *(expostulating)*. My dear Toop!

CLIVE *(quickly)*. What did you say?

BISHOP *(baffled)*. What?

CLIVE. I said, "What did you say?"

BISHOP. I—I—er—said nothing except. "My dear Toop"!

CLIVE *(groaning)*. Oooh! *(He swallows the brandy quickly.)*

BISHOP *(furiously)*. What have you done that for? *(The glass shakes in* CLIVE's *hand. Quickly.)* You're not going to faint, are you?

CLIVE *(miserably)*. No such luck. *(He hands the glass back to the* BISHOP, *whose hand shakes too.)*

BISHOP *(grumbling)*. Now I shall have to get some more.

CLIVE *(thirstily)*. Yes, get some more!

BISHOP. For Penelope!

CLIVE. Who? Oh, yes!

BISHOP *(furious)*. "Yes"! Well, upon my word! Such callousness is astounding! It's tantamount to slaughter.

CLIVE *(miserably)*. Oh, it can't amount to tantamount to slaughter.

(He crosses to R. *of* PENELOPE *and begins to fan her. The* BISHOP *goes for more brandy.)*

BISHOP *(as he pours brandy)*. What *is* the matter with everyone in this house? *(*IDA *enters with hot-water bottles and begins to ascend the stairs.* CLIVE, *seeing* *her, dives out of sight, R. of sofa. Seeing* IDA *on the stairs.)* Here, girl! Give me those.

IDA *(holding out the bottles)*. These, your Highness?

BISHOP. Yes. Give them to me and go! (IDA *hesitates. Taking the bottles.) GO!!* (IDA *goes off down* L., *quickly.)* We'll put these . . . *(He cannot see* CLIVE.) Now where . . . ? Toop! Where are you? *(He crosses and sees* CLIVE *on the floor behind the* R. *end of the sofa.)* Oh, there you are!

CLIVE. So I am!

BISHOP. What are you doing down there?

CLIVE *(rising and moving down stage a pace)*. I—er—I dropped last Sunday's collection.

BISHOP. WHAT????

CLIVE. Don't bother. *(Holding out a threepennybit.)* I've found it! Is she coming round?

BISHOP. Doesn't look like it. Get that brandy. I'll put these bottles at her feet.

CLIVE *(crossing L. for the brandy)*. Shouldn't she have a cold key down her back?

BISHOP *(dubiously)*. I don't know. It that usual . . .?

CLIVE *(quickly)*. Yes, of course it is! I know! You stay here and give her the brandy, and I'll run somewhere and see if I can find my uniform,—er—see if I can get a key.

BISHOP. There is no need for you to run anywhere. I have a key here. *(He produces a Yale key.)*

CLIVE. You would! The key of the poor-box? That's much too small. We'd have fun trying to get it back.

BISHOP. My dear Toop!

CLIVE. What! Now, you give her the brandy and I'll go and get the key of the vestry!

(He darts to the door down L. PENELOPE *moans.)*

BISHOP. Come back! It's all right. She's coming round. *(Above sofa.)*

CLIVE *(miserably)*. She would!

BISHOP *(moving to* C.) Come here! Come here!

Let her see you first! (CLIVE *crosses the* BISHOP, *and stands* R., *looking at* PENELOPE. L. *of the sofa, behind* PENELOPE'S *head*.) Go on. Say something!

CLIVE. What shall I say?

BISHOP *(irritably)*. Anything! Anything! Sing to her —it may soothe her.

CLIVE. Oh! *(Singing to the unconscious* PENELOPE.*)* "Some day I'll find you, Uncle's behind you!"

BISHOP *(furious)*. What are you talk . . . ?

CLIVE *(sees* PENELOPE *stir)*. Sh!!

PENELOPE *(opening her eyes—vaguely sitting up a little)*. Lionel! Lionel! Oh!! *(She faints.)*

CLIVE *(quickly, desperately and loudly)*. Pen, can you HEAR ME?

BISHOP. Don't shout at the poor girl like that! She's an indavid, not a long distance call! *(Testily.)* Oh! Get away from her. You have obviously no bedside manner. *(Bending over her face.)* Penelope, my dear.

PENELOPE *(coming round again, and seeing the* BISHOP *bending over her face from* L. *of the sofa.)* Lionel—Lionel! *(Then, with horror.)* UNCLE! Upside down! *(She falls back again.)*

BISHOP *(without any beside manner)*. Quick! The brandy!!! *BRANDY!* (CLIVE *crosses for the brandy and hands it to the* BISHOP. PENELOPE *revives, the* BISHOP *bending over her at* L. *end of the sofa.)* There, there, my child!

CLIVE *(behind him)*. There, there, my child!

(The BISHOP *glares at* CLIVE, *who retreats to the* R. *end of the sofa.)*

PENELOPE *(suddenly sitting up)*. How long does it take to get a divorce?

BISHOP⎰
CLIVE. ⎱ *(together)*. WHAT? ? ?

PENELOPE. How long does it take to get a divorce?

(CLIVE seizes her hand and begins to pat it vigorously.)

CLIVE *(wildly)*. THERE, THERE, MY CHILD! ! !

PENELOPE. Stop hitting me! *(Hitting* CLIVE's R. *hand.)*

BISHOP. Stop hitting her! *(Hitting* CLIVE'S L. *hand.)* Penelope, my dear, you are overwrought!

PENELOPE. I'll say I am!

BISHOP. What has this man done to you? *(He glares at* CLIVE.)

CLIVE *(speaking in the* BISHOP's *tone)*. I haven't done anything, have I?

BISHOP. Be quiet! I am addressing your wife.

PENELOPE. His wife! HIS!! ME . . . his!!

(CLIVE *and* PENELOPE *burst into peals of hysterical laughter.* CLIVE *sits on the hot-water bottles and leaps to his feet again.)*

CLIVE *(between his laughs)*. We should never have had that last gin and lime! *(He gives* PENELOPE *a playful push, which she returns, knocking him off the arm of the sofa into the fireplace.)*

BISHOP *(stunned)*. Gin and . . . ! So that's it!! Good heavens! You are both inebriated—drunk.

PENELOPE. Uncle——

BISHOP. No. I am shocked. Appalled. *(He crosses to the stairs and picks up his suitcase.)*

PENELOPE. Uncle— You're not going so soon.

BISHOP. I'm not going out. I'm going to bed. We will talk in the morning.

CLIVE. Now look here . . . *(Rises.)*

BISHOP. Not another word from you, sir! Penelope, which is my room?

PENELOPE *(rising)*. I'll show you.

BISHOP *(at the top of the stairs)*. You will stay where you are. I can find it myself.

PENELOPE *(moving to the foot of the stairs)*. It's the second on the left, and the bathroom is next to it. But, Uncle . . .

BISHOP. Thank you! Good night! Toop! It may interest you to know that a much-to-be-desired living has just fallen vacant in my Diocese. I came here hoping to find *you* the suitable person to fill the vacancy.

CLIVE. Oh, go away! Go away! *(He doubles up with laughter, at the fireplace R.)*

BISHOP *(speechless)* . . . I . . . ! Toop! I thought you were called to the Church, but apparently you were called to the Bar—— *(He exits upstairs, puts on pyjamas, robe.)*

PENELOPE *(coming down L.C., looking towards the closet L.)* Oh! *(Furiously.)* Oh, the rat! ! The unspeakable little rat!

CLIVE *(crossing below the settee to the L. end, R. of PENELOPE)*. Oh, I wouldn't call him a rat. Under normal circumstances. I'd say he was quite a cheery old soul.

PENELOPE. What *are* you talking about?

CLIVE. Your uncle.

PENELOPE. Well, I'm talking about my husband. *(Striding down to the door L. and returning to L.C.)* Oh! What am I going to do?

CLIVE. I will tell you exactly what you're going to do.

PENELOPE. I'm going to . . .

CLIVE. You're going straight upstairs to your dear uncle's room, and you will explain to him that he has made an absurd mistake—that I am NOT your husband, merely an old acquaintance. That your husband is a very good husband who at the moment . . .

PENELOPE. Who at the moment—*(pointing L.)*—is locked in the arms of a woman in that closet.

CLIVE WHAT??

PENELOPE. It's true, I tell you. Lionel is in there. *(Pointing.)* Locked in the arms of *that woman!*

CLIVE. What woman?

PENELOPE. There is only one "that woman" in my life—Miss Skillon.

CLIVE *(bewildered)*. But what are they doing in there?

PENELOPE *(shortly)*. Sleeping.

CLIVE. WHAT???

PENELOPE. He's in Miss Skillon's arms.

CLIVE. And what are you going to do about it?

PENELOPE. I'm going to get them both out of there and raise the devil! *(She starts towards the closet.)*

CLIVE *(seizing her arm to stop her)*. But how are you going to explain me away?

PENELOPE. I can't be bothered about that until I know what Lionel has been up to.

CLIVE. Well, while you're coping with that, I'd like my uniform. This situation calls for uniform.

(There is a sound of movement in the closet)

PENELOPE *(going to the closet and listening)*. They're moving in there. Hurry! I want to deal with them alone.

CLIVE. Once let me get that uniform on and I'll pass out of your life for ever.

PENELOPE. No, you don't. If I've got to explain you away to *Uncle*, I want you on the spot when I'm doing it! Now do go, please.

CLIVE. Well, give me the uniform, then.

PENELOPE *(opening the chest)*. Here it is. *(Looking in.)* No, it isn't!

CLIVE. Eh?

PENELOPE. It's gone!

CLIVE *What?*

PENELOPE. Gone!!

CLIVE *(diving into the chest, with a howl)*. What—the stripe as well?! Sergeant, Sergeant, have mercy on me!! *(Coming down stage* L.C. *with hands clasped.)*

PENELOPE *(tersely)*. Now then! Don't lose your head! *(Moving to the* L. *end of the sofa.)*

CLIVE *(moving to* L. *of her. Wildly)*. Lose my head? What does my head matter? I've lost my uniform, haven't I?

PENELOPE. For Heaven's sake, keep calm. We don't

know that it is lost yet, and even if it is you—you can easily buy another, can't you?

CLIVE *(burbling).* Buy . . . !!! *Buy another?* Give me strength not to hit you hard. How am I going to get back to camp without a uniform? Tell me that?

PENELOPE *(crossing him to down* L.C.). Use your imagination. Go as you are and bribe the Colonel to keep his mouth shut.

CLIVE *(at the* L. *end of the sofa).* Listen to the woman! *(Shouting.)* I want my uniform. Do you hear? I WANT MY UNIFORM!

PENELOPE *(moving up stage, and* L. *to* CLIVE). Will you stop shouting at me! You're not speaking to one of your brass hats now, remember! (CLIVE's *mouth opens, but he cannot speak.)* Really! If this is the sort of behaviour they teach you in the army, the sooner you resign, the better!

CLIVE *(with a groan).* Resign! Resign! Please! Please be quiet! Every remark you make is more stupid than the last! *(Bringing her down stage* C.) Get hold of that half-wit maid Ida from Idaho or whatever her name is. Ask her if she's seen it.

PENELOPE *(going up* R. *and looking off).* Why should she have seen it? *(Returning to* C.) And in any case, how am I going to explain how it came to be in the chest at all?

CLIVE *(down* L.C., *below the table).* I don't know and I don't care! All I know is, I want my uniform.

PENELOPE *(maddeningly calm).* I cannot understand how it got moved. Nobody ever goes into that chest— not once in a blue moon! There's nothing in it but tennis rackets and Lionel's golb clubs.

CLIVE *(piteously).* Woman, look! I am on my knees before you! *(He kneels.)* Don't, I beg of you, stand there pouring oil on an already blazing inferno! *Do something!* Get me my uniform!

PENELOPE *(moving away down* R.) Don't grovel about on the floor like that. You're taking all the crease out of Lionel's second-best trousers.

CLIVE (*following her on his knees, to* L.C. *below the sofa*). To hell with Lionel's second-best trousers! What about *my* trousers? Where are they?

PENELOPE. Listen! If the worst comes to the worst, I have an old kilt upstairs. Go back in that and say you've transferred to the Gordon Highlanders.

CLIVE. I want my uniform!

PENELOPE (*suddenly shouting*). If you say that again I'll hit you!

CLIVE. If you don't find it, I'll go straight upstairs and tell the Bishop everything.

PENELOPE. You wouldn't!

(*The* BISHOP *appears on the stairs wearing pyjamas and a dressing-gown.*)

CLIVE. Wouldn't I? Ha! He'd love to know the kind of man your husband really is!

BISHOP. He's learning, Toop! He's learning.

CLIVE (*prostrating himself, Moslem fashion*). Alms, Allah for the love of! Alms, Allah for the love of!

PENELOPE. Uncle, I thought you had gone to bed! (*She crosses up* C., *below* CLIVE, *who crawls on hands and knees to the* R. *end of the sofa.*)

BISHOP (*coming down* C.) I was almost in my bed when I heard someone shouting down here.

PENELOPE. We were just having a few words. That's all.

BISHOP. To me it sounded like a drunken brawl.

CLIVE (*leaping up*). Now look here, sir!

BISHOP. I am looking, sir!

CLIVE (*gloomily*). Don't bother!

(IDA *enters, down* L.)

IDA. 'Scuse me!

CLIVE. Oh, lor'! (*He slides out of sight behind the* R. *end of the sofa.*)

PENELOPE. What is it, Ida?

IDA *(confused)*. Could I have a word with you'm, alone?

BISHOP *(witheringly)*. Shall I go?

PENELOPE. No, of course not, Uncle.

BISHOP. I seem to be in the way.

IDA *(down* L.) It isn't your fault, your 'Ighness.

BISHOP *(exasperated.)* I do wish you wouldn't keep on saying that.

PENELOPE. Ida, will you go to bed?

IDA. But'm . . . !

PENELOPE *(sharply)* Bed!

IDA. Yes'm. Good night'm. Good night, Your Highness.

BISHOP *(roaring)*. Don't call me "Your Highness"!!

IDA. No, Your Greece, Your Grouse, Your Goose!

(She curtseys to the BISHOP *and exits hurriedly upstairs.)*

BISHOP *(testily)*. Penelope, I wish you would explain to that creature that I am neither the Archangel Gabriel nor the Aga Khan! And as for you, sir—— *(Looking round.)* Where has he got to now?

PENELOPE. Who?

BISHOP. Your husband. *(Crossing to below the sofa.)* Oh, there you are!

CLIVE *(sitting up)*. So I am!

BISHOP. As I came down the stairs just now, I could not help overhearing what you were both saying.

CLIVE *(muttering)*. We've got a sergeant like that.

BISHOP *(turning to* PENELOPE). Penelope, what are you hiding from me?

PENELOPE *(to down* C.) Nothing—nothing at all! We'll talk it over in the morning. Now do go to bed.

BISHOP. I will not go to bed until I know what is going on in this house. I heard this man distinctly say, "If you don't find it, I'll go upstairs and tell the Bishop everything." Now, what did he mean by that?

PENELOPE. Nothing—nothing at all! *(To* CLIVE.) *Did you, (with venom) dear?*

CLIVE. No—my sweet!

BISHOP *(to* CLIVE). And I suppose you meant nothing when you said, "He'd love to know the kind of a man your husband really is"?

CLIVE. Pen, please tell him the truth. Don't let him blabber on like this.

BISHOP. "Blabber," sir!

PENELOPE. Uncle . . .

BISHOP. No, Penelope! I am speaking to your husband!

PENELOPE. He's not my husband!

BISHOP. WHAT??

PENELOPE. He's not my husband! I'm not married to him!

BISHOP *(aghast)*. Not married . . . I think I'm going to faint! *There is a blood-curdling scream from* MISS SKILLON *in the closet.* PENELOPE *rushes to the closet door and stands with her back to it.)* Merciful heavens! What was that?

PENELOPE. I—I think it was an owl!

BISHOP. An owl?

CLIVE. Owl my . . .

BISHOP. Sir!

CLIVE. —foot. *(Crossing* C. *behind the sofa.)* Anyway, it wasn't an owl.

BISHOP. It sounded to me like a woman in distress. Was it someone in the house?

PENELOPE *(standing with her back to the closet door)*. Well, I thought it came from *outside. (She motions frantically to* CLIVE *to get the* BISHOP *outside.)*

CLIVE *(misunderstanding* PENELOPE'S *signals)*. What's the matter? Got something in your eye? Oh, *outside!*

BISHOP. No, I'm sure it came from inside. *(There is another scream.)* There it is again.

CLIVE *(suddenly)*. I know! The lily-pond.

PENELOPE. What?

CLIVE. The lily-pond. Someone must have fallen in the lily-pond.

PENELOPE. But we haven't got a lily-pond.

CLIVE. Of course we've got a lily-pond. Everybody's got a lily-pond. We must have a lily-pond. Come on, Bishop, we'll investigate.

BISHOP. But I'm not dressed for the lily-pond!

CLIVE. Lily won't mind. (He pushes the BISHOP *through the French windows*).

BISHOP. But it's cold out here.

(The BISHOP disappears.)

CLIVE Cold? All right, I'll get a fire. I won't be a minute. *(He closes the window and comes back into the room at c.)* Now it's up to you.

PENELOPE. What do you mean?

CLIVE. I'll keep the old man outside while you get your old man out of there.

PENELOPE. And then what?

CLIVE. Start praying.

(There is a loud HAMMERING at the closet door.)

MISS SKILLON. Let me out! Let me out! Aah!

PENELOPE *(putting her hands to her head in despair)*. Listen to that!

CLIVE. Let her out. Let them both out, or we shall have the Bishop thinking I'm murdering you.

PENELOPE *(opening the door)*. Come out!

(A very tousled MISS SKILLON emerges from the closet).

MISS SKILLON *(crossing to CLIVE and clinging to him hysterically)*. Oh! Oh! In there! In there! A man! Oh, Mr. Toop!!

PENELOPE *(to L.C.)*. Miss Skillon, please! Be quiet!

MISS SKILLON *(hysterically)*. How can I be quiet?

A man! *(In a feeble voice as she faints in* CLIVE's *arms.)*

CLIVE *(staggering under her weight)*. Oh, my Gosh!

PENELOPE. Miss Skillon!

CLIVE. It's no use shouting at her, she's fainted!

(The BISHOP *rattles the window.)*

BISHOP *(off)*. Open this window! Let me in! It's cold out here!

PENELOPE *(frantically)*. Oh, this is awful! What are we going to do? *(There is a loud ring at the front DOORBELL.)* Oh!

CLIVE. What was that?

PENELOPE. Someone at the front door!

CLIVE. NO!!!

PENELOPE *(shouting)*. YES!!

BISHOP *(off-rattling on the window)*. Let me in, I say!!

CLIVE *(quietly)*. I'm going mad!

(The DOORBELL rings again.)

BISHOP *(off)*. Open this window!!!!

CLIVE *(yelling towards the window)*. SHUT UP!!!

PENELOPE. Clive!!

CLIVE *(shouting)*. Stop "Clive"-ing me, or I'll throw Miss Skillon at you!

BISHOP *(off)*. What's going on in there?

CLIVE *(wildly)*. Aaah!

PENELOPE. Will you stop shouting?

CLIVE. No. I won't. I can't. I'm going mad. I tell you! get a straight-jacket! *(Drops* MISS SKILLON.*)* Call the wagon! *(Crosses* R.*)*

PENELOPE. Clive!

CLIVE. I'm seeing red! Tovarisch!

(In the meantime, LIONEL *has appeared in the closet doorway in a dazed condition, but on hearing*

CLIVE's *"Tovarisch"* he starts. He carries the poker in his hand.)

LIONEL *(pointing to* CLIVE). My assailant!
PENELOPE *(turning).* Lionel!⎱
CLIVE. WHAT?? ⎰ *(Together.)*
LIONEL *(wildly—raising the poker).* My assailant!
PENELOPE. Lionel, for Heaven's sake!
CLIVE. Pen, keep him off! *(He dodges* LIONEL *and runs around up* R., *and to the windows.)*
LIONEL *(rushing after* CLIVE). You shan't escape!
BISHOP *(off).* If you don't open this window I'll break it open.

(The DOORBELL rings loudly and continues to ring.)

PENELOPE *(to* CLIVE). Run, quickly. Run!
CLIVE *(rushing to the window and opening it).* I'm running. *(He leaps over* MISS SKILLON *and runs off down* L., *followed by* LIONEL.)

(The BISHOP *enters through the window, leaps over* MISS SKILLON *and rushes off after* CLIVE *and* LIONEL. PENELOPE *starts to pick up* MISS SKILLON *and* IDA *appears at the top of the stairs as—)*

THE CURTAIN FALLS

ACT THREE

SCENE.—*The same.*

TIME.—*A few seconds later.*

PENELOPE *is struggling with* MISS SKILLON, *who is helpless on the floor down* C. *Loud shouts from the garden. The front DOORBELL is still ringing loudly.*

PENELOPE *(calling wildly)*. Ida! IDA! *(Struggling.)* Ida, you must help me get Miss Skillon out of here.

IDA *(coming downstairs)*. Oh'm! I tried to tell you about her.

PENELOPE. Not now, Ida, please. Miss Skillon—get hold of her legs. (PENELOPE *is at* MISS SKILLON'S *head,* IDA *at her feet. They begin to lift her. A glass CRASH is heard in the garden.* PENELOPE *drops* MISS SKILLON. *She is now lying* C. *stage, parallel to the back wall and about six feet from the window. Rushing up to the windows.)* Oh! What are they doing out there?

IDA. Oh'm. They're 'aving the time of their lives—the dears! *(Peeping out of the window curtains,* R. *of* PENELOPE.) Ow—my goodness!

(IDA *is almost knocked over by* CLIVE, *who dashes in and goes off through the door down* L.—*leaping over* MISS SKILLON *in best steeplechase manner. He is followed by* LIONEL *who does the same business and exits. The* BISHOP *follows.)*

CLIVE *(as he "clears"* MISS SKILLON). Hi-di-hi!!

(Exit CLIVE, *followed, as above, by* LIONEL *and the* BISHOP.)*

62

IDA *(happily)*. "Ho-di-do." Boys will be boys, won't they'm? *(The* MAN *rushes in through the window. She sees the* MAN.) Ow! There's an "Also-Ran"!

(The MAN *leaps over* MISS SKILLON *and exits down* L. IDA *starts to move toward the door down* L.)

PENELOPE *(looking after him, blankly)*. Now . . . who could that be? Where are you going?

(The front DOORBELL has been ringing almost continuously.)

IDA. There's somebody at the front door'm.

PENELOPE. There has been for hours, but I can't ask anyone in here until we get Miss Skillon out of sight. *(She lifts* MISS SKILLON *into a sitting position on the floor.)*

IDA. You go to the door'm. I'll manage her. I've managed her quite a lot to-night.

PENELOPE. Shall I help you?

IDA. No'm. Off you go to the door. Give me a minute and I'll 'ave 'er out of sight.

PENELOPE. Thank you, Ida. *(She lets go of* MISS SKILLON, *who flops back on to the floor. DOORBELL.)* I'm coming! I'm coming!

(PENELOPE goes off down L.)

IDA *(lifing* MISS SKILLON *to a sitting position)*. Yo're a nuisance, that's what you are.

MISS SKILLON. Where am I? *(Seeing* IDA). *Ida!* What keeps happening to me?

IDA *(urgently)*. Listen! You've got to 'ide, do you hear? There's a bishop in the house. *(Helping her to her feet).*

(They stand down C., *with* IDA *on* MISS SKILLON's L., *supporting her.)*

MISS SKILLON. A bishop! He musn't see me here—not like this.

IDA. Here, this'll send you off to sleep. *(Taking the full glass of brandy from the table L.C.)* Now, back where you belong, and Ida'll make you a nice strong coffee to wake you up again.

MISS SKILLON *(pausing in the doorway)*. Ida! Tell the Bishop I am not at home.

(IDA puts her in the closet.)

PENELOPE *(putting her head round the door L.)*. Is it all right?

IDA *(quietly)*. All clear'm!

PENELOPE *(with false brightness)*. Come in! Do come in, won't you?

(PENELOPE enters, followed by the REV. ARTHUR HUMPHREYS. He is a mild little man. As he enters there is a wild, fiendish yell from the garden. HUMPHREY enters quickly as if pushed in the small of the back. PENELOPE rushes up to the curtains and peeps out.)

HUMPHREY. Thank you. Most kind. Most kind!

PENELOPE *(coming from the window)*. Not at all. Not at all. Have you been waiting long?

HUMPHREY *(politely, moving to down C.)*. A mere quarter of an hour.

PENELOPE. Splendid. I'm so glad. Do, *(she waves an arm vaguely)* won't you?

HUMPHREY *(after looking at her)*. Thank you. *(He moves up to the L. end of the table behind the sofa.)*

PENELOPE. Your hat. And your little scarf. *(She takes his hat, and then pulls off his muffler, almost strangling him, afterwards placing them on the table behind the sofa.)* Where is she, Ida? (IDA *points to the closet.)* Thank you, Ida, you've been most helpful. *(She waves her off.)*

IDA *(as she goes off into the kitchen—happily).* I thought you'd be pleased. *(She exits L.)*

PENELOPE *(to* HUMPHREY). Forgive me. I——

HUMPHREY *(down to the L. end of the sofa).* Not at all. It is I who must ask forgiveness. Arriving unexpectedly like this.

PENELOPE. It is perfectly all right, I assure you.

(A NOISE off. PENELOPE *moves a little to the windows.)*

HUMPHREY. But you must be . . .

(CLIVE *dashes in at the window, does a steeplechase leap at the place where* MISS SKILLON *was lying on his previous run through and exits down* L. HUMPHREY *watches him blankly.* PENELOPE *ignores him.)*

PENELOPE *(quite calmly).* You were saying?

HUMPHREY *(coming to with a start).* What? Oh! I was merely going to say that you must be surprised to see me.

PENELOPE *(vaguely.)* Oh no!

HUMPHREY. No?

PENELOPE *(murmuring).* What is one among so many? (LIONEL *dashes on* C. *and hesitates. Quickly to* LIONEL *as she points to the door down* L.) *That way!* (LIONEL *dashes off down* L.)

HUMPHREY. Mrs. Toop, if it will cause you inconvenience—my staying at the Vicarage—I will willingly go down to the inn in the village.

PENELOPE *(who has been peeping through the curtains).* That's very kind of you.

HUMPHREY. I—er—I—— My name, by the way, is Humphrey—Arthur Humphrey.

PENELOPE *(vaguely).* I'm sure it is. *(She steps aside quickly as the* BISHOP *dashes in. Pointing.)* That way!

(The BISHOP *disappears through the door down* L.

HUMPHREY *holds his head with both hands and sways a little. Then—recovering:)*

HUMPHREY. I—er—I . . . You see, Mrs. Toop—consulting a time-table, I discovered there is no train that would get me here in time for the . . . *(The* MAN *dashes on* C.—HUMPHREY *sees him and speaks automatically as he points). That way! (The* MAN *dashes off down* L.) . . . for the morning service.

PENELOPE *(looking towards the door down* L.). I wish I could place that one!

HUMPHREY. I beg your pardon?

PENELOPE. Nothing. I'm so sorry, I'm afraid I interrupted you. You were saying . . . ?

HUMPHREY *(desperately)*. Mr. Toop—could I see him?

PENELOPE. Mr. Toop? Oh, certainly. He's . . . round and about!

HUMPHREY *(to below the sofa)*. "Round and about." *(Turning to her)*. Mrs. Toop . . . You are Mrs. Toop, are you not?

PENELOPE *(moving up to the window—vaguely)*. More or less.

HUMPHREY. Is something troubling you, Mrs. Toop?

PENELOPE. Not a thing. *(A CRASH and SHOUTS off.)* Not a thing.

HUMPHREY. *(Sits sofa)*. But these—er—persons I saw running round the garden and dashing through the house . . . ?

PENELOPE. Oh! *(To down* C.). You musn't take any notice of that. That's just the—er—*Harvest Capers*.

HUMPHREY. Harvest Capers?

PENELOPE. Yes. It's a sort of game they play at harvest-time. Great fun. Would you care to join them?

HUMPHREY. No, thank you, no. I never caper.

(More SHOUTS off. HUMPHREY *starts.)*

PENELOPE *(rushing up to the window)*. Pity. Do you sing?

HUMPHREY *(surprised)*. No, Mrs. Toop, I'm afraid I don't sing. I recite a little at times, but I don't sing.

PENELOPE. Will you recite to me now?

HUMPHREY. Now? Well, Mrs. Toop, what shall I recite?

PENELOPE. Do you know "There are Fairies at the Bottom of our Garden."

(A loud CRASH and SHOUTS off. PENELOPE dashes out through the window and exits.)

HUMPHREY *(not noticing her departure)*. Well, Mrs. Toop, I'll do my best to recite "If" by Rudyard Kipling.

> "If you can keep your head when all about
>   Are losing theirs . . ."

MISS SKILLON *(from the closet)*. " . . . and blaming it on you."

HUMPHREY *(startled, but undaunted)*. "If you can trust yourself . . ."

MISS SKILLON. " . . . when all men doubt you."

HUMPHREY. Oh, Mrs. Toop! *(He looks round.)* Why, she's not here! Mrs. Toop! *(He runs first to the windows, then to the door up R. There is a KNOCK from the closet, followed by groans.)* Come in! Oh, there's something in anguish in that closet! Oh, he brave, Humphrey, be brave! *(He crosses L. and opens the closet and is just in time to catch MISS SKILLON in his arms as she falls.)* Goodness gracious, my dear lady, what has happened?

MISS SKILLON. Where is he? Where is he?

HUMPHREY. Where is who, Madam?

MISS SKILLON. That man, that dreadful man!

HUMPHREY. Don't you think you had better sit down for a moment?

MISS SKILLON. No. I must get away from this house. This wicked house! *(She crosses down R. to the front of the sofa.)*

HUMPHREY (*following her to* C.) Wicked? But, madam, this is the Vicarage!

MISS SKILLON. Vicarage or no Vicarage, I have been drugged!

HUMPHREY. What?

MISS SKILLON. Drugged!

HUMPHREY. Oh!

MISS SKILLON (*weeping*). *And* the Harvest Festival to-morrow! Oh, what will the harvest be? (*She collapses on to the sofa.*)

HUMPHREY. Bountiful, we hope. Dear lady, do sit down! Oh, you are sitting. Now tell me everything! (*He sits beside her.*)

MISS SKILLON. No, not everything.

HUMPHREY. Well, go as far as you can.

MISS SKILLON. Are we alone? (*She places her hand on his knee.*)

HUMPHREY. Now, now, now, now, now! (*Removing her hand.*)

MISS SKILLON (*replaces her hand on his knee*). Are we alone?

HUMPHREY (*again removing it*). Now! now! Now, you musn't do that.

MISS SKILLON. Where is Mrs. Toop?

HUMPHREY. Mrs. Toop? Well, she was here a moment ago. (*He rises and crosses up* L.C.)

MISS SKILLON. She musn't find me here. This is all her doing. (*Following him.*)

HUMPHREY. What is?

MISS SKILLON. My un-doing

HUMPHREY. But I don't understand. Who has . . . er . . . undone you?

MISS SKILLON. Take me away! *Take me away!*

(*She flings her arms round* HUMPHREY. IDA *enters down* L.)

HUMPHREY. Oh, Madam, please unhand me, I beg of you. Madam, I am a married man!

IDA (*to* MISS SKILLON). 'Ow did you get loose?

HUMPHREY. "Loose"!!

IDA. Trying 'er tricks on you, is she, sir? Don't take no notice of 'er. She isn't quite . . . well, you know. (*She taps her head significantly*).

HUMPHREY. Oh! Oh! I—er—— Good heavens. (*He leaps away.*)

MISS SKILLON. This is an outrage! (LIONEL *dashes in from down* L., *sees* MISS SKILLON *and rushes off again.*) It's him—I mean he! (*She screams, staggers past* HUMPHREY, *and faints into* IDA's *arms.*)

IDA. This is where we came in. (*To* MISS SKILLON.) Come on! Now in you go—— (*Business of getting* MISS SKILLON *in the closet.*) Back to your kennel. (*She closes the closet door.*)

HUMPHREY. (C.) But why do you put her in a closet?

IDA (*to* L *of him.*) Ow, she's a bad case, sir. 'As to 'ave darkness and lots of it. She's 'armless really, but "love-starved," if you know what I mean.

HUMPHREY. Quite. Quite! Tell me, who was the— person who rushed in here just now?

IDA. The less I say the better. There's things goin' on in this 'ouse that you wouldn't understand.

HUMPHREY. I can quite believe it! I have not understood a single thing that happened since I came here. (*He crosses down to the front of the sofa.*)

IDA. Would you like some coffee—while you're waiting like?

HUMPHREY. No. No coffee, thank you. But could you procure me a glass of milk?

IDA. 'Ot or cold?

HUMPHREY. 'Ot . . .

IDA. I'll get it right away, sir. (*At the door.*) An' whatever you see, pretend you didn't see. See? (*She exits* L.)

HUMPHREY (*sitting*). "Whatever I see, pretend I didn't see. See?

(PENELOPE *enters from the windows in time to catch* HUMPHREY's *line.*)

PENELOPE *(as she comes in—she is still very distrait).* Thank you so much. That was beautiful!

HUMPHREY *(dazed).* What was . . . ?

PENELOPE. Your recitation. Now, how about "The Wreck of the Hesperus"?

HUMPHREY. She's gone back to the closet!

PENELOPE *(as she moves from door to door, peeping out).* Oh! But I've disturbed you, just when you were going to have a little rest. Of course, you've had a long journey, haven't you?

HUMPHREY *(weakly).* Eight and three-quarter miles.

PENELOPE. Eight and three-quarter miles, and no dining-car! You must feel like a sodden rag. Now you put your feet up, and I'll mix you a pick-me-up.

HUMPHREY. But I don't want . . .

(PENELOPE *is now pouring whiskey, brandy and sherry at the table.)*

PENELOPE. Nonsense, of course you do! I always give this to all my friends. There! (CLIVE *rushes on c. Pointing with hand in which she has a glass of whiskey.) That way!* (CLIVE *crosses* PENELOPE *and as he does so takes the glass from her hand and exits French windows.* PENELOPE *is so distrait that she does not realize she no longer holds the glass. She crosses empty-handed to* HUMPHREY, *but her eyes are not on him.)* Now! Drink this. You'll soon feel better.

HUMPHREY. But I really don't . . . *(He starts as he sees* PENELOPE'S *empty hand extended towards him. He looks at her startled, then, convinced he is humouring a lunatic, says:)* Oh, well, just a little, perhaps. *(He pantomimes taking the glass and sipping a little.)* That was—er—delicious! I am not in the habit of . . . Oh! But I did enjoy that. The glass! Would you mind . . . ?

PENELOPE. The glass? *(He pantomimes handing the glass back.* PENELOPE *pantomimes taking the glass and returning it to the table.)* You feel better already, don't you?

HUMPHREY. Much! Much!

PENELOPE. I thought you might. Lie back and have a little nap. Nothing like a rest for sunstroke. *(Exits down* L.)

HUMPHREY. Sunstroke! They're mad! They must be!

(But PENELOPE *has disappeared through the curtains.* HUMPHREY *leaps to his feet and crosses to the table behind the sofa, picks up his hat, scarf and bag and makes for the French window. Enter* CLIVE.)

HUMPHREY ⎱ *(together).* ⎰ How you startled me, Mr.
CLIVE   ⎰   ⎱ Toop.

HUMPHREY (C., R. *of* CLIVE). Mr. Toop. I shall soon begin to think I am in a madhouse.

CLIVE. Well, you ought to know, it's your house, Toop.

HUMPHREY. Toop, this is the Vicarage, isn't it?

CLIVE. Why ask me, Toop?

HUMPHREY. Why do you keep calling me Toop Toop?

CLIVE. Well, aren't you Toop Toop?

HUMPHREY. No.

HUMPHREY ⎱ *(together).* My name is Humphrey.
CLIVE   ⎰

CLIVE. Oh, you're the *real* Humphrey. *(To down* R.C.) That's all right then. *(Turning.)* Have you seen a soldier's uniform?

HUMPHREY. A soldier's uniform? *(Moving down* C.) Here's another of them. Don't you think you ought to lie down for a few moments? You must be tired after your capers in the garden.

(PENELOPE *enters down* L.)

PENELOPE. Oh, there you are.

CLIVE. My uniform? *(Crosses to* PENELOPE) No. I just mistook that for your old man.

(HUMPHREY *crosses up* R., *and puts down his hat and scarf.)*

PENELOPE. How dare you!

CLIVE. Sorry *(looking at his clerical clothes)*, but the same lodge.

PENELOPE. Where is Uncle? *(Crosses up L. and C.)*

CLIVE. Uncle? Oh, Uncle! The last time I saw him he was taking a "header" into a gooseberry-bush.

PENELOPE. Go and dig him out at once.

CLIVE. I was going to sit down for a few moments.

PENELOPE. *(up C.)* You were going to *what?*

CLIVE *(indicating* HUMPHREY*)*. Our friend here seemed to think it advisable. *(To* HUMPHREY.*)* Didn't you?

HUMPHREY. Well, I certainly thought you appeared a little—er—unstrung.

(IDA *enters* L., *with a glass of milk on a tray.)*

IDA. 'Ere we are, sir.

CLIVE *(quickly, to* HUMPHREY*)*. Excuse me! *(He dives out of sight behind the sofa, at the* R. *end.)*

IDA *(crossing to* HUMPHREY*)*. 'Ere we are, sir!

HUMPHREY *(crossing* L.C.*)*. Thank you. *(He takes the milk.)*

IDA *(crossing to the* L. *end of the sofa, peering over it—to* CLIVE*)*. What do you want to keep doing that for?

CLIVE *(rising—miserably)*. H'm?

IDA. What you want to 'ide for, every time I come into the room?

CLIVE. You bring out the gypsy in me.

IDA. You can trust your little Ida. Ida won't squeal.

PENELOPE. Ida, you may go!

IDA. Yes'm. *(To* CLIVE.*)* I like you better in your uniform.

CLIVE. Oh, good! *(Starting.)* By the way, you haven't seen it, of course?

IDA. Of course. *(She crosses to the door* L.*)*

CLIVE *(despondently)*. Of course. *(Then, starting.)*

Does that mean of course you haven't or of course you *have? (He follows her to the door.)*

IDA. Of course I 'ave!

CLIVE *(yelling)*. You have? Where is it?

IDA. It's in my kitchen.

CLIVE *(a slight burst of hysterical noises)*. In her kitchen. *(He turns to* HUMPHREY, *who is, of course, convinced that* CLIVE *is mad. At* L.C.) Did you hear? It's in her kitchen! "In her kitchen."

HUMPHREY. So I gathered!

IDA. I took it there for safety.

CLIVE *(wildly)*. Ida, I love you!

PENELOPE (L. *of the sofa)*. Oh, for heaven's sake be quiet! Ida, go and bring *it* in here.

IDA. Yes'm.

PENELOPE. At once.

IDA. Yes'm. *(At the door—to* CLIVE.) He loves me. *(She exits.)*

PENELOPE *(to* HUMPHREY*)*. You musn't take any notice of Ida, she's just a little—well, you know, but a splendid worker.

HUMPHREY. Mrs. Toop . . . You *are* Mrs. Toop, are you not?

PENELOPE. That's one thing I *am* certain of.

HUMPHREY. I cannot help feeling that my presence in your house is an embarrassment to you. Have I your permission to find accommodation for the night in the village?

PENELOPE. Of course, I just don't know how to begin to apologize to you for——

CLIVE. Why not tell him everything? You're a sportsman, aren't you?

HUMPHREY. Well, I never got a blue for anything. But I'm very good at rounders.

CLIVE. Rounders? You must come and join us sometime.

HUMPHREY. Mr. Toop—you are Mr. Toop, are you not?

PENELOPE *(crossing to* R. *of* CLIVE L.C.). *That's* just

it. As a matter of fact, my husband is just outside—
and will be here in a minute.

CLIVE WHAT? ? ?

PENELOPE. He's . . . *(There are SHOUTS from the
garden, then the* MAN *rushes wildly into the room,
through the windows. To* CLIVE—*not noticing the*
MAN's *entrance.)* Why don't you go and help Uncle
find him?

HUMPHREY *(down* C., *turning to face the* MAN *at
the windows).* Ah, Mr. Toop, at last!

(The MAN, *thinking* HUMPHREY *is about to attack him,
gives him a blow on the chin.* HUMPHREY *falls on his
back—unconscious. The* MAN *dashes down below*
CLIVE *and* PENELOPE *and off down* L.)

PENELOPE *(crossing to the door* L.) Isn't it infuriat-
ing when you can't place a face?

CLIVE. Never mind about facing a place—placing a
face! *(He unconsciously strides over* HUMPHREY.)
Where on earth is Ida with my uniform?

PENELOPE. Oh! I don't know. *(Becoming aware of*
HUMPHREY *on the floor.)* Oh, look at this dear little
man!

CLIVE *(turning, at up* R.C.) Why?

PENELOPE *(looking down at* HUMPHREY). What *is*
the matter with him?

CLIVE *(after a cursory glance).* He's tired.

PENELOPE. He's unconscious!

CLIVE. He's lucky.

PENELOPE. We can't leave him like this—strewn all
over the floor.

CLIVE. Well? Have you got a vacuum cleaner? *(Already lifting* HUMPHREY—*irritably.)*

PENELOPE. He's coming round. *(She crosses to the
table* L.C. *and pours a drink.)*

HUMPHREY *(opening his eyes).* Where am I?

CLIVE. Did you *have* to say that?

PENELOPE *(bringing the glass to* CLIVE). Give him
this.

CLIVE *(to* HUMPHREY*)*. Here! Drink this!

HUMPHREY *(waving the drink aside)*. Air! Air!

CLIVE. He doesn't want this. *(He drinks it himself and hands the glass to* PENELOPE.*)* He wants some air. *(To* HUMPHREY.*) With* soda? Oh, *AIR!* I know what you mean. *(Leading* HUMPHREY *to the window.)* I think we've got some out in the garden. Come along—this way.

PENELOPE. What? Where are you going?

CLIVE. Back to the lily-pond.

(He exits with HUMPHREY.*)*

PENELOPE. Don't give up hope. Remember, as one door closes another opens. *(She moves to and opens the door down* L. *The* MAN *is standing on the threshold.)* Oh! Do come in!

(The MAN *enters, quickly closes the door, stands with his back to it—hand in pocket.)*

MAN. Listen! I am a desperate man!

PENELOPE. I'm not exactly carefree!

MAN *(Crosses* C. *Follows)*. Do you know who I am?

PENELOPE. My dear, I've been trying to place you all the evening.

MAN *(crossing her to* C.*)* Out there in the garden there are men—hunting for me.

PENELOPE. What? Oh, no! you're mistaken. It isn't you they're after. It's . . .

MAN. *I* tell you they are hunting in your garden for me.

PENELOPE *(with a shrug)*. Well, they've got a nice night for it. *(The* MAN *produces a revolver.)* What on earth! Put that thing away; it might be loaded.

MAN. It is loaded.

PENELOPE. "It is loaded." What?!

MAN. Be quiet. If you value your life you must help me.

PENELOPE. But . . .

(A NOISE in the garden.)

MAN. They are here. *(He forces* PENELOPE *over to the sofa.)* Sit down!

PENELOPE *(sitting* R. *end of the sofa).* Look here——

MAN *(menacingly—with revolver).* I am your *husband.* You understand?

PENELOPE *(wildly).* Oh no! I remember him.

MAN. Your husband—*or your life! (He sits* L. *of her.)*

(CLIVE *and* HUMPHREY *enter at the windows.)*

CLIVE *(as they enter—brightly).* There, there, my child!

MAN *(to* PENELOPE). If you betray me . . .

PENELOPE *(to* HUMPHREY). Are you feeling better now?

HUMPHREY. (L. *of* CLIVE). I—I—— *(To* CLIVE.) You say you are *not* Mr. Toop?

CLIVE. You're not going to start that all over again.

PENELOPE *(after a quick look at the* MAN). No. no, of course he isn't Mr. Toop. *(Pointing to the* MAN.) Er —this is Mr. Toop.

CLIVE *(startled).* What?

PENELOPE. I said this was Mr. Toop. *(To the* MAN.) Aren't you, darling?

MAN. Yes.

CLIVE. Oh! *(Moving down* R.C.) Well, I'm glad to meet you, darling . . . I mean . . . I say! You move pretty quickly, don't you?

MAN. Huh!?

CLIVE. Not five minutes ago you were running round the garden in your underwear, and now here you are clothed and in your right mind—if one could be in **this house.**

PENELOPE *(to the* MAN*)*. You're like that, aren't you, darling?

MAN. Like what?

PENELOPE. Dressed to-day and stripped to-morrow.

HUMPHREY *(coming down* L. *of* CLIVE.) Mrs. Toop, have I your permission to . . .

PENELOPE *(with a wave of the hand)*. Yes, certainly. Second door on the left.

(HUMPHREY *is silenced. During the following dialogue he quietly picks up his hat, coat, bag, etc., with the intention of stealing out of the house.)*

CLIVE *(to* PENELOPE*)*. Your husband—have you told him about—er—— *(He points to himself and* PENELOPE.*)* And has he told you about—— *(Pointing to the* MAN *and the closet.)*

PENELOPE *(hurriedly)*. Oh yes! Yes! It was all a joke, wasn't it, my sweet?

MAN. A yoke—— Yes!

CLIVE. A yoke!! You call it a yoke to run around in your underpants?

PENELOPE. Of ceurse it was. *(Miserably.)* Ha-ha!

(HUMPHREY *is stealing out of the doorway,* L.)

CLIVE. A yoke! Now where have I heard that before . . . *(To* HUMPHREY.*)* Whither away, friend?

(HUMPHREY *spins round.)*

HUMPHREY. I—I—— Where can I wash?

CLIVE. All over if you like, but before you go—— *(Dragging* HUMPHREY *into the room.)* Do *you* think it's a yoke to run around the garden in your underpants?

HUMPHREY. I have never run around a garden in my underpants.

(LIONEL, *in underpants, dashes in down* L., *crosses in*

front of CLIVE *and* HUMPHREY, *then upstairs.* CLIVE, *clutching* HUMPHREY, *gapes after the departed* LIONEL. PENELOPE *is very agitated.* LIONEL *changes to clerical clothes.)*

CLIVE *(to* HUMPHREY, *quietly).* Just HOW mad are *you?*

HUMPHREY. I don't know—I was perfeltly sane when I entered this house.

CLIVE. I'm wondering if you thought you saw what I thought I saw?

HUMPHREY *(wretchedly).* What do you think you thought you saw?

CLIVE. *I* think I thought—— *(Desperately.)* Did a pair of underpants run up those stairs just now?

HUMPHREY. They did, but they were . . . er . . . in-habited.

CLIVE. Did you see them?

PENELOPE. Yes.

CLIVE. Who was it?

PENELOPE. The Vicar.

CLIVE *(swings round on* PENELOPE). You just told me that he was the Vicar. *(To the* MAN.) Who are you? Don't lie! You're not! *(He moves towards the* MAN).

MAN *(springing to his feet).* Stand back!

CLIVE. What?

MAN. Do not move, any of you!

CLIVE. Here! What the . . .

MAN *(producing revolver).* The first one to move a step will get a bullet through the head.

HUMPHREY. But, Mr. Toop . . .

PENELOPE *(wildly).* This is *not* my husband.

HUMPHREY *(baffled).* Not?

PENELOPE *(almost shouting).* NO!!

HUMPHREY *(definitely shouting.)* But you said just now that he WAS!

CLIVE *(slapping* HUMPHREY's *hand.)* Don't bicker,

Vicar! *(To the* MAN.) Now look here, old man—a yoke's a yoke, but—— *(He moves a step towards the* MAN).

MAN. If you move a step . . . Do svidan ya! *(Dahs-vee-TAWN-ya.)*

CLIVE. Do svidan ya? He's a Commie!

HUMPHREY. What?

CLIVE. A Red!

PENELOPE. No! !

CLIVE. Yes, he is! *(Very quickly.)* Watch! Tovarisch! *(He gives the Red salute quickly.)*

MAN *(quickly and automatically).* Tovarisch!

(He also gives the salute, but quickly recovers his former position.)

CLIVE You see! He couldn't resist it.

MAN. One more example of your clerical humour, my friend, and it will be your last.

CLIVE. Oh, indeed. *(Moving towards him.)* Why, you no good little .   .

PENELOPE. Don't!

CLIVE. Perhaps you're right.

HUMPHREY. This is dreadful.

CLIVE. *But* dreadful!

HUMPHREY. Er—— What are we going to do?

CLIVE. I don't know.

HUMPHREY. We must think!

CLIVE. Let's try that, shall we?

MAN. The key to the garage——

PENELOPE. You're going to take my car?

MAN. I am.

PENELOPE. You won't get far, there's no gas.

MAN *(doubtfully).* Is that so?

CLIVE. Yes, we've just filled our lighters! I say . . . do you mind if we sit down? We've had rather a strenuous evening.

MAN. No tricks.

CLIVE *(mildly)*. Hi Ho! *(He sits* L. *of the table* L.C.*)* Do sit down, old boy.

HUMPHREY. *(down* L.*)* I—I don't feel I want to sit down . . . somehow.

MAN *(fiercely)*. Sit down! *(He moves to* R.C.*)*

HUMPHREY. Yes. *(He flops quickly on the stool down* L.*)*

CLIVE. Now! Where do we go from here?

MAN. What?

CLIVE. We can't just sit here like this, can we?

MAN *(crossing to* C.*)* Listen to me. Outside there are soldiers looking for me.

CLIVE. Soldiers?

MAN. Yes.

CLIVE. That's lucky.

MAN *(backing up* C.*)* It is lucky for you that you are not a soldier or you would be dead by now.

CLIVE. What, me—a soldier? Oh, very funny, ha ha! *(He tries to pull his trouser legs over his army socks.)*

(Enter IDA, L.*)*

IDA. Here it is, sir. Here's your uni——

CLIVE *(jumping up)*. Not now. Take it away.

(He bundles her out and slams the door.)

MAN *(from the window)*. Come back. If any of those men come in here you are to pass me off as one of yourselves.

CLIVE. Oh, I couldn't do that— My sergeant would be livid.

MAN. I can see that you are going to be troublesome. Perhaps the lady and I can carry off the deception better—alone.

HUMPHREY. Er—how are you going to—er—dispose of *us?*

MAN *(after looking wildly round the room—pointing to the closet).* What is through that door?

PENELOPE. It's—it's just a closet.

MAN. *You (to* CLIVE) and you *(to* HUMPHREY), in you go!

HUMPHREY. But I—er—I—think that particular closet is engaged.

MAN. Who is in there?

CLIVE. Sweet Rosie O'Grady!

MAN *(fiercely.)* In you go. At once! *(He threatens them with the revolver.* CLIVE *and* HUMPHREY *move over to the closet reluctantly.)* Stop! *(They stop by the closet).* Now listen to me very carefully. If anyone comes into this room you are not to make the slightest sound. The lady and I will be close together. (PENELOPE *creeps to the telephone, but he stops her.)* Stop that! *(To the* OTHERS.) She will be covered with this revolver. If you attempt to raise an alarm in any way, a bullet will enter her heart. Understand?

CLIVE. I think so!

PENELOPE *(anxiously to the* MAN). Perhaps you'd better repeat it.

CLIVE *(to* PENELOPE). Chin up, sweetheart.

HUMPHREY. "Sweetheart"—Ah! then you are Mr. Toop? *(They shake hands.)* I'm so glad to meet you!

CLIVE. What? Oh! How do you do?

MAN. In you go. (HUMPHREY *opens the closet door and goes in. To* CLIVE.) And you?

CLIVE. Look here! You can't do this to me!

MAN *(sticking the revolver in his ribs).* Can't I?

CLIVE *(looking at the revolver).* Of course you can. *(To* HUMPHREY.) Step to the rear of the bus. *(Exits.)*

MAN *(returning to* C.) First of all I want some money.

PENELOPE. Money?

MAN. For my escape.

PENELOPE. I'll write you a check.

MAN. I want money now. You must have some in the house. Where is it?

PENELOPE. It's in my bedroom. *(As a thought strikes her.)* I'll get it.

MAN. WE will get it. *(VOICES off stage.)* Too late. They are here!—Remember! I am your husband. *(He forces her back to sit in the sofa.)* Between us we will soon get rid of them. Your name. What is it?

PENELOPE. Penelope.

MAN. Penelope what?

PENELOPE. Toop! You don't think you'll get away with this do you?

MAN. I sincerely hope so, for your sake!

(VOICES are again heard off stage.)

BISHOP *(off)*. There is no need to go round to the front door. There's a window here.

SERGEANT. All right. All right.

MAN. Who is that? *(Alarmed.)*

PENELOPE. My uncle.

MAN. Your uncle? Then he will know that I am not your husband. He will betray me, and I shall have to shoot you!

PENELOPE. I believe you're just aching to shoot me. If you will keep quiet, I think I can manage to save my own skin.

MAN *(firmly)*. And mine?

SERREANT *(off)*. Orl right . . . orl right! *(The MAN goes down R., behind PENELOPE. A very dishevelled BISHOP enters through the windows with SERGEANT TOWERS, a cockney, in the uniform of a British Sergeant. MAN sits on sofa. SERGEANT as they enter.)* Nuffink to get excited about!

BISHOP *(entering to L.C.)* I am *not* excited, but I tell you that man of yours deliberately knocked me down on to that marrow-bed.

SERGEANT *(to L. end of the sofa)*. 'E was only doin' his duty for his King and Country. 'E thought you was the bloke we're after, see? 'E thought you was the Russian spy.

BISHOP. But I tell you . . .

SERGEANT *(cheerfully).* 'An any'ow, 'ow do I know you're not, eh? You 'aven't proved it yet, 'ave you, pal?

BISHOP. Pal ! ! ! Penelope! Will you please tell this gentleman who I am? *(He crosses to L. of the table and sits.)*

PENELOPE. Of course, darling. *(To the* SERGEANT.*)* Sergeant, this is my uncle, the Bishop of Lax!

SERGEANT *(gasping at the* BISHOP*).* A Bishop! Oo 'ell! Sorry, yer Bishopric, no offense!

PENELOPE. What happened to you, Uncle?

SERGEANT *(helping himself to a drink).* Well, yer see, mum, it's this way. We're lookin' for a Commie spy that's escaped from the Guard House, see. So we has a scout round and comes across the old geyser here —no offence, sir, upside down in a gooseberry-bush, see? His legs was sticking up and at first we thought he was a wheelbarrow.

PENELOPE. Well, I can assure you, Sergeant, my uncle is not the man you are looking for.

SERGEANT. Oh, well, that's that. I suppose you haven't seen a stranger knockin' about, mum?

PENELOPE. No, I'm afraid I haven't.

SERGEANT. Oh well, that's that. *(Moving up stage to peer out of the French windows.)*

MAN. Get rid of them.

PENELOPE. What?

MAN. Get rid of them.

PENELOPE. Uncle, dear, why don't you go to bed? You've had a very busy evening, you know. Sergeant, will you be round here long?

SERGEANT *(coming down* C.*)* We're bound to 'ang about until we find 'im. But don't you worry.

PENELOPE. I'll try not to.

SERGEANT *(having finished his drink and going up* C.*)* Well, I'll be off. Good night, all! *(Opening the curtains a little.)* What a lovely moon, makes me feel all romantic.

BISHOP. Are you married, Sergeant?

SERGEANT. Why bring that up? *(He exits through the windows.)*

BISHOP *(rising, and coming* C.*)* Now, Penelope, I should like a full explanation, and I presume this is your husband?

PENELOPE. Yes, Uncle, this is my husband. *(Hurriedly.)* Lionel dear, this is Uncle Dudley. *(Flounderingly.)* You . . . you've heard me speak of him.

MAN *(rising)*. Tovar—!

(PENELOPE *kicks his ankle, the* MAN *sits quickly.)*

BISHOP *(dazed, but holding out his hand)*. How do you . . . *(Seeing his hand is ignored.)* Oh! But I don't understand. If this is your husband, who was the man who kept on hiding?

MAN *(aside to* PENELOPE*)*. He was the Russian!

PENELOPE. He . . . He was the Russian!

BISHOP. WHAT???

PENELOPE. The Russian!

BISHOP. You mean the man those soldiers out there are hunting for? Then why didn't you tell me before?

PENELOPE. You see, all the time he was here, he had me covered with a revolver.

BISHOP. My poor child! No wonder you behaved so strangely. Then who was the person I mistook for a lunatic?

PENELOPE. That was you, wasn't it Lionel?

MAN. Yes.

BISHOP. But why were you in a state of—er—er—undress?

PENELOPE. Yes, Lionel, why were you? Tell Uncle.

MAN. The Russian came in here when I was alone. He attacked me and took my clothes.

BISHOP. My dear children, what a ghastly experience. *(To the table above the sofa.)* Suppose we telephone the police? What do you think?

MAN *(rising)*. I think it would be most unwise. *(He moves down* R.*)*

BISHOP. Do you? Why?

(He is stretching out his hand to take off the receiver, but hesitates, as the MAN *turns to face him.)*

MAN. Before the receiver had left the hook your lifeless body would, no doubt, be falling to the floor!

(The BISHOP *leaps away from the telephone quickly.)*

BISHOP *(to* C.*).* My dear Toop, please! Must you express your conjectures quite so . . . so . . . melodramatically? *(Murmuring.)* "My lifeless body . . . !" *(Moving to* L. *of the sofa.)* I think, if you don't mind . . . *(He indicates the brandy bottle.)* I feel the need of a little stimulant.

PENELOPE. I'll get you one.

(She rises and crosses to the table, the MAN *at her heels.)*

BISHOP. Why do you follow your wife around like this?

MAN *(unemotionally).* I love her!

BISHOP *(blankly).* A most abnormal passion. *(*PENELOPE *crosses and hands him a drink. She and the* MAN *march back to the sofa and sit. There is a distinct CRASH from the closet.)* Penelope! There is something in that closet! *(He moves up towards the closet.)*

PENELOPE *(who is on the* R. *of the* MAN: *wildly).* No, Uncle, No, Uncle, no! It's nothing. Just the cat!

BISHOP. The *cat?*

PENELOPE. Yes, darling. It's Tiddles sleeping in there. She's slept in there for years.

BISHOP. Then it's time she came out! *(He moves to the closet door.)*

MAN. Stop him or I shoot!

PENELOPE. Uncle! Don't open the door.

BISHOP. Why not?

PENELOPE. It might be dangerous.

BISHOP. Dangerous? Why?

PENELOPE Dangerous . . . why? . . . oh!—She's going to have kittens!

BISHOP. Oh, I love the little things. *(To down* L.) I wonder how many she'll have?

MAN. I am tired.

PENELOPE. Tired? I'm exhausted.

MAN. Shall we go to bed?

PENELOPE. Yes, *(Rising—then sitting quickly.)* Certainly not.

MAN *(in an undertone).* The money.

PENELOPE. What?

MAN. The money.

PENELOPE. Oh, yes—very well. I'll get some for you. *(They rise, and march towards the stairs. At* R. *of the stairs, they check, and* PENELOPE *turns to the* BISHOP, *who is peeping through the keyhole of the closet door. Blowing a kiss to the* BISHOP.) Good night, my poppet.

MAN. Good night, my poppet. *(He clicks his heels and gives a Russian bow.)*

(They exit up the stairs. The BISHOP, *left alone, peeps through the closet keyhole.* IDA *enters* L. *She is carrying* CLIVE'S *uniform. As she sees the* BISHOP *she starts—moves to* C., *and conceals the uniform behind her back.)*

IDA. What are you doing in that closet, Your Highness?

BISHOP. I was just going to have a look at the old cat.

IDA *(moving up stage a little).* Oh, I wouldn't do that. She's tiddley.

BISHOP *(to* C.). I wonder if she's *had* her kittens?

IDA. Had her what? You're upset, and no wonder, after the frolicking round you've had to-night. Been kinda' taken out of yourself, 'aven't you?

BISHOP *(crossing below* IDA *to* R.C.) Yes, and the sooner I'm put back the better.

IDA. Would you like Ida to get you a nice plate of cold Spam?

BISHOP. I ask for nothing more than a few biscuits.

IDA. They're in the dining-room. I'll get them for you.

BISHOP. Don't bother. I would prefer to choose for myself.

(He exits to the dining-room, R.)

IDA *(calling after him)*. Not much choice, I'm afraid. We've only got two sorts. Whole or broken. *(She looks round the room.)* Now where's 'e gone? I can't lug this uniform about all night. *(She has an idea. She puts the uniform back in the chest, goes to the window and calls.)* Mr. Whatsyername—Corporal—are you out there? *(She exits through the French windows.)*

(CLIVE enters from the closet, L.)

CLIVE *(calling)*. Yes, Ida, I'm here! *(Going to the window.)* Ida, are you there?

(The BISHOP re-enters R. Seeing a man's back, he concludes it is LIONEL.)

BISHOP. Oh, I thought you'd gone to bed (CLIVE *turns round.)* The Russian!

CLIVE. No. My name is Humphrey.

BISHOP. Humphrey?

CLIVE. Yes. I've come to take the Service to-morrow.

BISHOP. You're an impostor sir! You have no right to be wearing those clothes at all.

CLIVE. Oh, you know, do you?

BISHOP. Yes. You've changed your camp and escaped from your uniform.

CLIVE. No. My uniform escaped from me. I know where it is now. In the kitchen.

(He goes towards the door down L.)

BISHOP. Come back, sir!

CLIVE. Sorry, I'm in rather a hurry. *(He exits.)*

BISHOP *(moving C., calling after him)*. Come back, sir!

(LIONEL enters from upstairs, wears clerical suit.)

LIONEL. Oh, are you Mr. Humphrey?

BISHOP. No, sir. Aren't you?

LIONEL. No, I'm Toop.

BISHOP. You're an impostor.

LIONEL. I beg your pardon. Who are *you?*

BISHOP. I am the Bishop of Lax.

LIONEL. Then it is you who are an impostor, for I happen to know that the Bishop is not arriving until to-morrow.

BISHOP. I tell you I am the Bishop of Lax. And I happen to know that I've arrived to-night. *(He adds as an after-thought.) An*d I happen to wish I hadn't.

LIONEL *(to himself)*. Oh dear, where is Penelope?

BISHOP. Penelope has gone up to bed with her husband.

LIONEL. WHAT!!!! *(He starts towards the stairs. PENELOPE enters on the stairs, attended by the MAN.)* Penelope!

(They walk straight past the OTHERS towards the sofa.)

BISHOP. Where are you going?

PENELOPE *(down R.)* For a walk.

BISHOP. But you just went up to bed because you were tired.

MAN (L. *of* PENELOPE). I have insomnia

BISHOP *(to R.C.)*. That's no reason why Penelope should go for a walk.

PENELOPE. He likes me to go everywhere with him. don't you, darling?

LIONEL *(dropping down* L.C.) Darling? But, Penelope——

BISHOP *(firmly, pointing to* LIONEL). Penelope, who is this man?

PENELOPE. That? Oh that's Mr. Humphrey.

BISHOP}
LIONEL} *(together).* Mr. Humphrey?

(Enter HUMPHREY *from the closet to* C.)

HUMPHREY. Did anyone call?

(Enter CLIVE *down* L.)

CLIVE. It isn't there.

(The SERGEANT *enters through the window, carrying the* MAN'S *uniform from ACT II under his arm. The* BISHOP *looks round amazed. The room appears to be filled with clergymen.* CLIVE, HUMPHREY, LIONEL *and the* MAN *(still close to* PENELOPE*) all gaze at each other in astonishment.)*

SERGEANT (C.), Wot's going on 'ere? Eh? *(Seeing all the clergymen.)* Blimey! *(Counting 1, 2, 3, 4.)* One, two, three, four. What's this? The crow's nest?

*(*CLIVE *and* HUMPHREY *watch the* MAN *make a definite movement near* PENELOPE.)*

BISHOP. Sergeant, arrest most of these people!

SERGEANT. Most of 'em?

PENELOPE. Uncle, if only you'd keep quiet.

BISHOP. Well, who are all these people? They can't all be Mr. Humphrey.

SERGEANT *(kindly).* Now you pipe down, Your Bishopric, and I'll ask the questions. *(Not so kindly.)* Sit down, everybody. (LIONEL *brings the chair up* L. *down to the table. They* ALL *sit, except the* BISHOP

and the SERGEANT. CLIVE *on the stool down* L., HUMPH-
REY L. *of the table* L.C., LIONEL *above the table,*
PENELOPE *and the* MAN *on the sofa.)* Now then! One
of my lads found these in the garden just now—the
clothes the Russian was wearing when he 'opped it.

LIONEL *(rising).* I must speak.

SERGEANT. Sit down. Now it stands to reason that if
he's got rid of these, 'e must be wearing clothes that
don't belong to 'im.

CLIVE. *If* he's wearing any clothes at all!

SERGEANT. Shut up. An' as these was found in a
Vicarage garden, it's as likely as not that he's wearing
a suit of clothes wot he's pinched off the Vicar.

HUMPHREY. Most probable . . . *(Seeing the* SER-
GEANT'S *eye on him.)* I'm so sorry. Don't let me inter-
rupt.

SERGEANT. I won't! *(Heavily.)* So wot we 'ave to
look out for is a man dressed like a parson.

CLIVE *(nervously covering his clerical collar with his
coat lapels).* Yes . . . er . . . Yes, he's quite right.

SERGEANT *(ponderously as he looks at the four
clerics).* A man dressed as a parson.

(The FOUR MEN *look embarrassed.)*

HUMPHREY. But good heavens, Sergeant, surely you don't suspect . .

LIONEL. If I may be allowed to speak . .

CLIVE. Now look here, old boy . . .   *(together)*

BISHOP. Sergeant, you are quite right
in your . . .

MAN *(to* PENELOPE.) You are still
covered.

SERGEANT. 'Alf a minute! 'Alf a minute! This isn't
a Parish Council Meeting.

*(*IDA *enters down* L.)*

IDA. 'Scuse me!

SERGEANT *(spinning round, startled)*. Who the 'ell are you?

IDA *(on her dignity)*. I BEG yours? *(She crosses to L. of the* SERGEANT *at* C.)

PENELOPE *(agitated)*. This is Ida, my maid.

SERGEANT. Your maid, eh?

PENELOPE. Yes, what is it, Ida?

SERGEANT *(heavily to* IDA). So you're the maid, are you?

IDA. Not very quick on the uptake, are you? *(She waves him aside.)* Could I 'ave a word with you, mum, alone?

(CLIVE, *on* IDA'S *entrance, has been struck with an idea. He pulls a ten-shilling note out of his pocket and, unseen by* OTHERS, *scribbles on the back of it.)*

SERGEANT. No, you can't. Nobody leaves this room till I give the word.

IDA *(alarmed)*. Why, what's happened?

SERGEANT. Never you mind, my girl. Out you go, and thank your lucky stars you're not mixed up in it— or *are you? (Looking* IDA *up and down—then witheringly.)* No! You couldn't be!

IDA *(as she crosses down* L. *to the door)*. Oh dear, what 'ave you been up to, all of you?

(CLIVE *rushes up to* IDA, *seizes her hands and forces the ten-shilling note into* IDA'S *hand.)*

CLIVE *(dramatically)*. Good-bye, Ida, there's ten shillings for you.

IDA. But you've written . . .

CLIVE. No, don't thank me now. One word of advice before you go. Look at the money twice before you spend it. Quickly.

(IDA *exits flustered.)*

SERGEANT. Now which of you lot is the vicar 'ere?

LIONEL. I am.

BISHOP *(pointing to the* MAN*)*. He is.

MAN. Me.

HUMPHREY *(pointing to* CLIVE*)*. This gentleman.

*(All the answers come more or less simultaneously.
There is a slight pause, then:)*

SERGEANT *(heavily)*. I shall repeat my question. *(A
pause.)* Which of you—if any—is the vicar 'ere? *(They
ALL repeat their answers, this time together.)* Blimey!
(He moves down R.*, looking at them from side to side.)*
I shall repeat my question just once more. *(In a sinister,
low voice). Which of you is the Vicar 'ere? (Complete
silence.)* So you won't talk, huh? *(A pause.)* Lost your
tongues now, 'ave you? *(He moves up to behind the
sofa.)*

HUMPHREY *(testily)*. My good Sergeant . . .

SERGEANT *(sharply)*. Now then! Now then! None of
your soft soap.

CLIVE *(to* HUMPHREY*)*. Humour him, old boy, humour him. Call him "General." Ask him what he did
at Ladysmith.

HUMPHREY. What did you do to Lady Smith?

SERGEANT *(spinning round)*. 'Ere, what's this—
what's this? You two in this together, eh?

CLIVE. Good Lord, no!

SERGEANT *(pointing to* HUMPHREY*)*. Is 'e the vicar
'ere?

CLIVE. No. . . I . . . *(To* HUMPHREY.*) Are* you the
"vicar 'ere"?

HUMPHREY. You know very well I'm not.

SERGEANT. 'Ow does he know that you're not?

HUMPHREY. Because *he* is the vicar 'ere.

LIONEL. I protest.

BISHOP. Sergeant, I must point out that the obvious
way to find out who is the vicar is to ask his wife. *(He
points to* PENELOPE.*)*

SERGEANT. Well, there's something in that. *(To* PENELOPE.) Now, mum—I suppose you *are* the vicar's wife?

PENELOPE. Yes, Sergeant.

SERGEANT. Well, which of this lot is your husband?

PENELOPE *(after a look at the* MAN—*pause)*. This is my husband.

LIONEL *(aghast)*. Wh . . . what? ? ? ? THAT IS A LIE!

SERGEANT. Eh?

LIONEL. *I* am my wife's husband! *(To* PENELOPE.) Penelope, have you gone mad? I tell you I am the vicar of this parish and this lady is my wife.

SERGEANT. Then why doesn't she say she is?

LIONEL. Penelope, for Heaven's sake tell this man the truth.

CLIVE. Ah. Truth will out. That's what I always say. *(To the* SERGEANT.) What do you always say?

SERGEANT. Shut up.

CLIVE. I've noticed that.

SERGEANT *(to the* BISHOP). Your identification card, if you please.

BISHOP. I do not carry my identification card in my pyjamas.

SERGEANT. Defaulter number one. Your identification card, if you please.

LIONEL. It's in my other suit.

SERGEANT. Defaulter number two. *(To* HUMPHREY.) Your identification card, if you please.

HUMPHREY *(pointing to the cover of a magazine)*. So that's Betty Grable! I must have left it at home. Very naughty of me.

SERGEANT. Very. Defaulter number *three*. *(To* CLIVE.) Your identification card . . .

CLIVE. If you please. Believe it or not, Sergeant, I am the ghost of Hamlet's father. I have not got my identity card.

SERGEANT⎱
CLIVE   ⎰ *(together)*. Defaulter number four.

SERGEANT. A comic parson, eh? Well, you don't make me laugh. *(To the* MAN.) Your identification card.

MAN *(producing the card from his pocket)*. Certainly, Sergeant.

SERGEANT. Blimey! He's got one! *(He takes the card and examines it. Reading.)* "Toop, Lionel, The Vicarage, Merton-cum-Middlewick."

LIONEL. You villain! That is *my* card! That is my identification card. *(Pointing to the* MAN.) Those are my clothes. That man knocked me down and took them from me.

SERGEANT. What? Why didn't you say so before?

LIONEL. Because I didn't recognize him. But that card proves it.

MAN. That is precisely what happened to me. I was attacked and my clothes were taken. I told you about it, didn't I, Bishop?

BISHOP. What? Oh, yes! Yes! *(He moves up above the sofa table.)*

SERGEANT *(in a low voice of baffled fury, as he sweeps the* MEN *with a look of utter contempt)*. You low-down, double-crossin' bunch of . . .

CLIVE. "Baskets"—we know!

(There is a general uproar.)

SERGEANT. You're under arrest—the whole lot of you!

(More uproar. Suddenly the loud clanging of church BELLS tops the fresh outburst.)

PENELOPE. What on earth . . . ?

SERGEANT. Lor' Lummy! *(Goes to French windows.)*

BISHOP. A conflagration!

LIONEL. A what! (ALL *go to windows.)*

HUMPHREY. A conflagration!

MAN. A conflagration? This is the final conflagration. Do scidan ya! *(Levels revolver.)* Our leaders have kept their word! At last, at last! Capitalist swine! Soon you will be crushed by the Iron Curtain. Soon the British bulldog, the British Empire, the British . . .

CLIVE *(Moving to him)*. Gas Light and Coal Co.

MAN. . . . Gas Light and Coal Company . . . All . . . ALL shall perish. *(With a flourishing gesture.)* This is . . .

CLIVE. The Revolution!

MAN. The Revolution! Tovarisch! Tovarisch! *(He gives the salute with the hand holding the revolver, and* CLIVE *tickles him under the armpit. The* MAN *drops the revolver.)*

CLIVE *(picking up the revolver and handing it to* LIONEL*)*. Take this and keep him covered.

LIONEL *(waving the revolver wildly)*. Stand back, everyone! How does this thing work?

*(*EVERYONE *dodges.* CLIVE *snatches the revolver from* LIONEL *and hands it to the* SERGEANT.*)*

SERGEANT *(to* HUMPHREY*)*. Hey, you!

HUMPHREY. Me?

SERGEANT. Run round the garden, see if you can find any of my men and tell 'em to come 'ere right away. Go on! RUN!

HUMPHREY *(going up to the windows)*. Oh, certainly! I'm not terribly good at running, but . . .

SERGEANT. RUN! (HUMPHREY *exits through the windows, followed by* CLIVE. LIONEL *goes down* L. *The* SERGEANT *covers the* MAN.*)* Wot I can't understand is why you didn't tell me 'oo he was right away.

PENELOPE. Well, Sergeant, what would you do with a revolver tickling the ribs?

SERGEANT. You mean 'e . . . ?

PENELOPE. Yes, Sergeant. MY ribs!

SERGEANT *(to the* MAN*)*. You . . . dirty Commie!

PENELOPE. That reminds me. You won't be wanting the housekeeping money now. *(She crosses to the MAN and takes a wad of notes from his pocket. Then crosses down L. to LIONEL.)*

LIONEL. Oh, my darling! No wonder you behaved so strangely!

SERGEANT *(to LIONEL)*. Your "darling"? Then you *are* the vicar 'ere?

LIONEL. I am!

SERGEANT. Glad to meet you! You might ring up the police an' tell 'em we've got our bird!

BISHOP. I'll do it. *(He lifts the 'phone receiver.)*

SERGEANT *(to the MAN)* Come on, Tovarisch! Behind the Iron Curtain!

(The SERGEANT and MAN exit through the windows.)

BISHOP. Give me the Police Station, Merton-cum-Middlewick, please.

LIONEL. Are you all right, Penelope?

PENELOPE. Yes, I think so. It was rather a shock, but I'm all right now.

LIONEL. I'm so glad, my dear. You know, I think I ought to go and find out who it was ringing the bell. *(He exits down L.)*

BISHOP. *Is* that the Police Station, Merton-cum-Middlewick? Bah!

PENELOPE. Wasn't it?

BISHOP. No, the Odéon, Leicester Square. *(He exits R. to the dining-room.)*

(CLIVE enters C.)

CLIVE. Quickly—before they come back! My uniform!

PENELOPE. Ida told you it's in the kitchen.

CLIVE. But it's not. I've looked.

PENELOPE. Everywhere?

CLIVE. Everywhere.

PENELOPE. Then let's start all over again at the chest.

CLIVE. Why waste time looking in the one place where we know it isn't? (PENELOPE *opens the chest and picks out the uniform. Hugging it to his chest.*) Oh, you darling thing, I never thought I'd be so pleased to see you. Quick there's somebody coming! *(He hastily embraces* PENELOPE *and repeats:)* Oh, you darling thing. I never thought I'd be so pleased to see you. (PENELOPE *thrusts the jacket into* CLIVE's *arms, keeping the trousers. Enter* IDA. C.) Oh, it's only Ida.

IDA. Are you all right, mum?

PENELOPE. Yes, thank you, Ida. Did you hear the church bells?

IDA. Hear 'em? I rung 'em!

PENELOPE. What do you mean?

IDA. Well, he wrote on the ten-bob note, "ring church bells."

CLIVE. And the trick worked. The ruddy Red thought it was the signal for the Communist Revolution.

PENELOPE. Oh, so that's why he changed his tune.

CLIVE. Talking of changing—I'd better go in here again. *(He opens the dining-room door.)*

BISHOP *(off).* Is that you, Ida?

(IDA *exits down* L. CLIVE *shuts the door quickly.*)

PENELOPE. Uncle's in there. You'd better go upstairs, and when you've changed——

CLIVE. Just jump out of the window. Don't forget I've got to get out of here as soon as possible. *(He exits upstairs.)*

(Enter the BISHOP *from the dining-room up* R.)

BISHOP. Are there any more biscuits in the kitchen?

(Enter LIONEL *down* L.*)*

LIONEL. Penelope, it was Ida who——

(Enter MISS SKILLON *from the closet.)*

MISS SKILLON. I won't stay in there one moment longer.

LIONEL. Miss Skillon, haven't you gone home yet?

MISS SKILLON. No, but I am leaving your house this instant.

PENELOPE. That's the best news I've had to-night.

MISS SKILLON. Mr. Toop, you have horrified me. Mrs. Toop, you have only confirmed the opinion I have always held of you.

LIONEL. Miss Skillon, you may be one of my oldest parishioners, but I cannot stand here and let you besmirch my wife's character.

MISS SKILLON *(with a sniff.)* Character? Huh!

LIONEL. Yes. She may be a trifle more broad-minded than we are, but . . .

*(*CLIVE *enters at the top of the stairs. He has changed his clerical jacket for the upper half of his uniform, but is still wearing black trousers.)*

CLIVE. Penelope, have you seen my trousers?

MISS SKILLON. Trousers? *(She turns to* PENELOPE *and sees the trousers on her arm.)* Ah!!! *(She turns again to* CLIVE.*)* Why, surely . . . *(Then with horror.)* Yes, it is!

LIONEL. What is?

MISS SKILLON *(pointing at* CLIVE*)*. Mrs. Toop's sweetheart!

PENELOPE. Really!

LIONEL⎱ *(together).* WHAT??
BISHOP⎰

MISS SKILLON. The soldier in the Jeep. And it **was**

YOU having the rough and tumble on the carpet with Mrs. Toop!

LIONEL. WHAT???

MISS SKILLON. Yes! I thought it was *(to* LIONEL) you, but it was *(to* CLIVE) YOU. How did you come by those clothes?

LIONEL. Penelope, what does this mean?

BISHOP *(coming down below the sofa.)* I SHOULD like to know what EVERYTHING means.

CLIVE. We'd better tell them.

PENELOPE. Yes, I suppose we'd better. Look, Lionel, you sit there. *(She puts* LIONEL *in the chair* L.C. *The* BISHOP *sits on the sofa).* You see, Lionel—Clive——

CLIVE. I'm Clive. How do you do?

LIONEL. Oh, how do you do?

(They shake hands.)

PENELOPE. He's an old friend of mine.

CLIVE.. Very old!

PENELOPE. We toured together . . .

CLIVE⎱ *(together)* ⎰In a play called
PENELOPE⎰   ⎱"Private Lives."

BISHOP. One of you at a time, please!

PENELOPE. Well, you see, Lionel, after you had gone this evening Clive turned up here.

CLIVE. And, as we were very old friends, Pen suggested we should go out together.

PENELOPE. And I saw in the Blatford paper that the Little Theatre there was playing . . .

PENELOPE⎱ *(together).* "Private Lives"!
CLIVE ⎰

PENELOPE. . . . So I suggested we should go and see it.

(Meanwhile CLIVE *crosses front of stage to* L. *of the sofa, and continues telling the story to the* BISHOP, *while* PENELOPE *continues telling* LIONEL.*)*

CLIVE. You see, I haven't seen Penelope
since—until to-night. I'm in the army now,
stationed at Wathampton. I saw Penelope
yesterday when I was passing through the
village in a Jeep. This evening, I thought
I'd look her up. I called here. We were
wondering how we might spend the evening, when Pen saw in the local paper that
the local Company was playing "Private
Lives."

PENELOPE. You see, Lionel, after you'd *(together)*
gone this evening, Clive turned up here.
He's stationed at Wathampton. As I was
alone in the house, I thought it best for us
to go out somewhere—I saw in the Blatford paper that the Group there were playing "Private Lives," so I suggested that
we should go and see it. As Blatford is out
of bounds for Clive, I lent him your
second-best suit.

CLIVE *(to* PENELOPE). How far have you got?
PENELOPE. Second-best suit. Where are you?
CLIVE. "Private Lives," but I'll catch you up!

CLIVE. Of course we had to see it again,
but as Blatford is out of bounds for me, I
couldn't go in uniform, so Pen lent me
(crossing to LIONEL) *your* second-best
suit. We were just going off when an argu-
ment cropped up about the play, where Pen
and I had a fight—stop me if I'm going too
fast. It's a very tricky fight. And while we
were doing it Miss Skillon must have come
into the room.   *(together)*

PENELOPE. You see, Lionel, if Clive had
gone in uniform he might have been shot
and his seven days' leave stopped. Of
course if I'd had the slightest idea that
you (crossing to the BISHOP) were going
to arrive to-night, Uncle, I should never

have dreamed of going.—You do follow what I'm saying, don't you? Well, just as we were ready to go, we began arguing about a scene in the play where Elyot— that's Clive's part, and Amanda—that's my part—have a terrific fight.

BISHOP. *(Knocking his head with clench-ed fists.)* I shall go mad in a minute!

LIONEL. I cannot understand a word of all this!

(together)

CLIVE. You see, we were both on the floor—like this. *(He grabs PENELOPE and they both fall on the floor and fight.)* While we were doing this Miss Skillon——

PENELOPE. You see, we're both on the floor like this—— *(She is dragged to the floor by CLIVE.)*

(together)

MISS SKILLON *(coming forward).* Yes?

(CLIVE and PENELOPE repeat the business at the end of Act I from PENELOPE's line.)

PENELOPE. Beast; brute; swine; DEVIL! *(She again lands out with a stinging blow. Again MISS SKILLON gets it full in the face, and falls back into IDA's arms. PENELOPE and CLIVE fall away, leaving MISS SKILLON and IDA C.)* and *that's* how it all began.

CURTAIN.

SEE HOW THEY RUN

FURNITURE PLOT

Act 1

Carpet.
Sofa R. by the fireplace, facing the audience.
Table above the sofa.
Round table down L.C.
Armchair L. of the round table.
Chest up L.C. by the stair banisters.
Armchair between the chest and the French windows
Floor lamp behind the armchair.
Closet L. of the door up R. (facing the audience).
Occasional table down R. below the fireplace. Mirror
    over.
Stool below the door down L.
Curtains at the french windows (open).
Pictures.

PROPERTY PLOT

Act I

On Stage.—On the occasional table down R:
    Vase of flowers.
  Newspapers, including the local paper open at the
    cinemas.
  On the closet:
    Vase of flowers.
    Ashtray.
    Matchbox with match ready.
  Inside closet:
    Smelling salts.
    Bottle of cooking-sherry, ¼-full.

On the table behind the sofa:

    Telephone, R. end.

    Ashtray.

    Silver cigarette-box with 3 cigarettes.

    Matchbox with match ready (front edge of the table).

    4 magazines, including "Film Pictorial."

On the round table L.C.: Silver tray with silver tea-pot (full), silver jug of milk, muffin-dish with muffin (quartered), 2 cups, saucers, spoons (stacked).

    Silver cigarette-box with 5 cigarettes.

    Ashtray.

    Matchbox with match ready.

    Lady's cigarette-case (empty).

    2 copies of "Punch" and other magazines.

In built-in closet L.: Toop's hat, coat, muffler (on back of the door).

    Clothes-brush and clerical hat (on pegs on backing).

    Clerical suit, folded (on the chair).

Off Stage L.C. *(on Rostrum).*—Compact and lipstick (PENELOPE).

    Clerical suit, folded (PENELOPE).

    Clerical collar and bib (PENELOPE).

Personal Property.—REV. LIONEL TOOP—Pocket-watch.

ACT II

Strike clerical hat, clothes-brush, compact, lipstick, cigarette case, 2 magazines from the table R.C.

Reset cushion on the armchair L. of the table L.C.

Reset local paper on the table down R.

Set cushion on L. arm of the sofa.

Set wooden tray with 5 tumblers on the table L.C.

Set sherry bottle (uncorked) and 1 tumbler on the table behind the sofa (for MISS SKILLON).

Off Stage.—(R.): Paper (the MAN).

    (L.): Bottle of whiskey and bottle of brandy (un-

opened) (REV. LIONEL TOOP).
2 hot-water bottles (IDA).
Suitcase (BISHOP).
Small key (BISHOP).

ACT III

Strike hot-water bottles.
Set tumbler ½-full of whiskey R. edge of the table L.C.
Set bottles of whiskey, brandy and sherry on a tray on
    the table L.C.
Off Stage L.—Small gladstone and white scarf
    (HUMPHREY).
  Glass of milk on salver (IDA).
  Wad of notes, revolver, identity card (the MAN).
  Clive's uniform (IDA).
  10s. note and pencil (CLIVE).
  Denim uniform (SERGEANT).
  Notebook and pencil (SERGEANT).

SEE HOW THEY RUN

COSTUMES

IDA: Maids uniform, later changing to garish suit and funny hat. *(Cockney accent)*.

MISS SKILLON: Tweeds, necktie, felt hat, heavy walking shoes.

REVEREND TOOP: Clerical suit and collar, coat and hat. Later appears in white shirt and athletic shorts.

PENELOPE: First entrance wears dressing gown, later changes to slacks and blouse; spring coat. *(American)*.

CORPORAL CLIVE WINTON: *(American)* Uniform of Air Force Corporal; later changes to clerical suit, bib, hat. *(This is a quick change during action and must be carefully rehearsed)*.

INTRUDER: Wears blue denim dungarees and jacket *(kind used as Navy Fatigues)* marked with large letter "P" in white. Later changes to clerical costume.

BISHOP OF LAX: Clerical costume; later changes to pajamas or night-shirt, and bathrobe, slippers.

REVEREND HUMPHREY: Clerical costume.

SERGEANT TOWERS: Cockney. Can wear either British army uniform, or British police uniform as desired.

(NOTE: Five Clerical costumes, all black, are required.)

SEE HOW THEY RUN

EFFECTS PLOT

Act I

1. Door-bell.
2. Telephone-bell

Act II

3. Telephone-bell.
4. House-bell.
5. Bumping (R.).
6-11 Door-bells.
12. Door-slam.
13. Bumps in closet L.
15-20. Door-bells.

Act III

21. Door-bell.
22. Glass-crash and shouting.
23. Door-bell.
24. Door-bell.
25. Door-slam, glass-crash and shouting.
26. Glass-crash and shouting.
27. Glass-crash and shouting.
28. Bumps in the closet L.
29. Church bells.

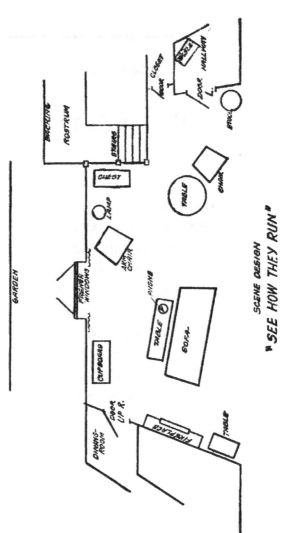

GARDEN

BACKING

ROSTRUM

STAIRS

CLOSET

DOOR KNOB

CLOSET

DOOR

BEDROOM

STOOL

CHEST

TABLE

CHAIR

LAMP

ARM CHAIR

DOOR

FRENCH WINDOWS

DOOR

CUPBOARD

TABLE

PHONE

SOFA

DOOR U.P R.

DINING-ROOM

FIREPLACE

TABLE

SCENE DESIGN

"SEE HOW THEY RUN"

Also By

Philip King

BAD BAD MOUSE

ELEMENTARY, MY DEAR

GO BANG YOUR TAMBOURINE

HERE WE COME GATHERING

I'LL GET MY MAN

MILK AND HONEY

MURDER IN COMPANY

ON MONDAY NEXT

POOLS PARADISE

SAILOR BEWARE!

WATCH IT SAILOR

WHO SAYS MURDER?

THE DECORATOR
Donald Churchill

Comedy / 1m, 2f / Interior

Marcia returns to her flat to find it has not been painted as she arranged. A part time painter who is filling in for an ill colleague is just beginning the work when the wife of the man with whom Marcia is having an affair arrives to tell all to Marcia's husband. Marcia hires the painter a part time actor to impersonate her husband at the confrontation. Hilarity is piled upon hilarity as the painter, who takes his acting very seriously, portrays the absent husband. The wronged wife decides that the best revenge is to sleep with Marcia's husband, an ecstatic experience for them both. When Marcia learns that the painter/actor has slept with her rival, she demands the opportunity to show him what really good sex is.

"Irresistible."
– *London Daily Telegraph*

"This play will leave you rolling in the aisles....
I all but fell from my seat laughing."
– *London Star*

OTHER TITLES AVAILABLE FROM SAMUEL FRENCH

CAPTIVE
Jan Buttram

Comedy / 2m, 1f / Interior

A hilarious take on a father/daughter relationship, this off beat comedy combines foreign intrigue with down home philosophy. Sally Pound flees a bad marriage in New York and arrives at her parent's home in Texas hoping to borrow money from her brother to pay a debt to gangsters incurred by her husband. Her elderly parents are supposed to be vacationing in Israel, but she is greeted with a shotgun aimed by her irascible father who has been left home because of a minor car accident and is not at all happy to see her. When a news report indicates that Sally's mother may have been taken captive in the Middle East, Sally's hard-nosed brother insists that she keep father home until they receive definite word, and only then will he loan Sally the money. Sally fails to keep father in the dark, and he plans a rescue while she finds she is increasingly unable to skirt the painful truths of her life. The ornery father and his loveable but slightly-dysfunctional daughter come to a meeting of hearts and minds and solve both their problems.

OTHER TITLES AVAILABLE FROM SAMUEL FRENCH

TAKE HER, SHE'S MINE
Phoebe and Henry Ephron

Comedy / 11m, 6f / Various Sets
Art Carney and Phyllis Thaxter played the Broadway roles of
parents of two typical American girls enroute to college. The
story is based on the wild and wooly experiences the authors
had with their daughters, Nora Ephron and Delia Ephron,
themselves now well known writers. The phases of a girl's life
are cause for enjoyment except to fearful fathers. Through the
first two years, the authors tell us, college girls are frightfully
sophisticated about all departments of human life. Then they
pass into the "liberal" period of causes and humanitarianism,
and some into the intellectual lethargy of beatniksville. Finally,
they start to think seriously of their lives as grown ups. It's an
experience in growing up, as much for the parents as for the
girls.

"A warming comedy. A delightful play about parents vs kids. It's
loaded with laughs. It's going to be a smash hit."
– *New York Mirror*